How to Keep (and L♥ve) Your Long Distance
Relationship: Advice for the Modern-Day Couple With
Distance Woes

How to Keep (and L♥ve) Your Long Distance Relationship: Advice for the Modern-Day Couple With Distance Woes

A v a R e y

To the boy I love most, Tyrone.

Dedication

Intro: Relationship Facts: Long Distance Edition

....

Part 1

....

Part 2

....

Part 3

....

Part 4

....

Part 5

....

....

....

Relationship Facts: Long Distance Edition

....

Relationships are fucking hard. Anyone that says otherwise has never been in a heart-tugging, fact-finding, tear-jerking, stare-into-your-eyes-forever, it's-my-way-or-the-highway relationship.

In other words—the only relationships that matter.

So, yes, relationships are hard. So hard, in fact, that according to The Washington Post[1], over seventy percent of new couples will break up within the first year in any regular short-distance relationship (you know, the kind with face-to-face conversations, hour-long fights, make-up sex, cuddling, and all around spending time together), let alone a *long distance relationship* (you know, the kind *without* that contact—the good or the bad—that face-to-face we love so much, the physical needs of the average warm blooded mammal).

Are you ready for some depressing facts? Well, here you go: According to a study conducted May 14, 2016 by Statistic Brain[2], there are fourteen million couples who consider themselves to be in a long distance relationship in the United States.

Oh, you think you read that wrong? I'll say it again: fourteen *million* people in the United States of America are in long distance relationships. Fourteen million!

I knew I was crazy the moment I started mine, but I certainly didn't expect millions of people to be just as crazy as me. But love is love and the heart wants what the heart wants. Or so they say.

Out of those millions of couples, forty percent will break up within the first four and a half months, and seventy percent will break up if the relationship is stagnant and unchanging.

That's a staggering amount of breakups.

Sorry. It's statistics.

I told you it would be depressing.

Here's more juicy (depressing) information. Average distance of couples in a long distance relationship is 125 miles, 2.7 days between phone calls, 1.5 visits per month, and a whopping fourteen months for the average couple to move closer together. That's pretty freaking depressing.

Whatever happened to live by the seat of your pants, fall in love, move cross country chasing love, life, learning and living, and what about living for the *experience*? Caution, that's what happened. Not surprising given the amount of failed close distance relationships and high divorce rates.

So, what do the fourteen million of us have to look forward to? Fourteen months of lonely nights and wishful daydreams? Nuh uh, no siree. Long distance relationships don't have to be boiled down to statistics and might-be's. Those of us in long distance relationships know there's more than statistics and distance.

There's so much more.

Read on, fellow lovers, romantics, fighters and optimists, because no matter what kind of relationship you find yourself thrown into, trust, hard work, dedication, compromise, and unconditional love are the basis of a successful relationship. Phone sex may be the answer to all long distance couples' prayers, but trust me, it doesn't even begin there, fun as it may be (unless you have thin walls and a roommate).

How to Keep (and Love) Your Long Distance Relationship: Advice for The Modern-Day Couple With Distance Woes is about surviving your long distance relationship and what to expect from one.

Relationships are fucking hard whether your better half is close by or far, far away. The ride is not going to be easy, but it's going to be *fucking fun*.

Chapter 1

Meeting in Las Vegas
(New York, Tokyo, Toronto or Anywhere Because Cupid's Arrow Flies Everywhere)

....

So you met once while walking down the coveted Strip you hardly ever go to because you're over the glitz and the neon, but your helpful friends made you go in an attempt to get you out of that rut that's been keeping you bitchy and more than a little irritable. It has been three months since your last bf, and let's face it, you get cranky when you don't get any on the regular, and let's also admit you're not into one nighters—unfortunately. But give a girl enough tequila, and who can blame you for reenacting spring break circa 2008?

You've had your rebounds, regretted them all and resolved to being that crazy lady (ahem, twenty-something, thank you very much), with three cats and an armadillo named Pooky (another poor decision, but now you're stuck with the critter until it dies and that's that), when the stars align, fireworks blast off, and those pretty birds from the Disney movies you grew up watching lead you to *The One*. And man, is he a *man*.

With an Eiffel Tower tumbler full of green alcoholic slushy in one hand, and a camera in the other, you know right away. He's the one. And when his glossy eyes meet yours, you swoon and lose your shit, because how is he even real? That's why. Beard of Zeus, different colored eyes—one blue one brown, just like in Practical Magic, *but in real life—*and the plumpest lips you've ever seen since Lucious Lips back in high school when life was great and your only problem was getting into a good college. Your legs are shaking as you stare at The One, your lips trembling, and let's not even mention your cooch—which has gone unnoticed for far too long, yet awakened by this Greek god of lust and desire.

He walks towards you with a cool stride, or so he thinks. You're smiling as he comes closer and introduces himself and you swoon like you swore you never would. Your girls notice his guys and all of a sudden it's a freaking party while you're trying to contain your dancing heart. You make it to a dance floor and his scent mixes with yours and it's all over. Pheromones attack you and refuse to let you go. You're sweaty, and he loves it.

You think you've found the one.

You got it bad, and it's only the beginning.

◆ *Reminder:* Sometimes meeting people in person can be so overrated. Sometimes all we have to do is swipe right to find The One, and sometimes, that person just happens to be miles and miles away. So if you've met your boo in person or online, the premise is still the same. Maybe a few emails were exchanged when you fell—and fell deep—maybe it was texting that did you in, or maybe it was liking each others selfies on Instagram. Love comes in all shapes, sizes and in all forms, so don't fret! Skyping your boo can be just as intimate as a candle-lit dinner.

◆ *Hot Tip*: Meeting online can bring you so much closer. I mean, there's no initial awkwardness because there can't be. It's all sifted out in the very early stage of meeting. You don't keep the conversation going when it's dull and you certainly don't keep trying if it's clear he ain't shit. So if it's going strong, it's most likely all witty texts, pretty selfies, and hearing each other's voice for the first time. It's a big—HUGE—rush, and the distance makes it so much safer to be yourself. Conversations get deeper sooner and it starts getting real. So be real. Chances are you're both talking to a few people you swiped right for, so be yourself and stand out from the skanks. You have nothing to lose and everything to gain.

Chapter 2

Getting to Know Prince Charming: AKA, the Fun Part

....

There's nothing quite so picturesque as the infatuation stage of a relationship. The world is tinted pink, and clouds are made of cotton candy as you skip into the fairy-tale sunset with your new conquest. You can't get enough of his conversation, or the way he touches your hand in the car, the way he looks at you during dinner—like he just wants to throw you down and go at it—and you want to spend every minute with the guy. It's like everything he says is covered in chocolate—Swiss chocolate. Melted Swiss chocolate. It's like you're the strawberry and he's the melted chocolate that covers you in decadence.

His jokes make you laugh, his driving doesn't make you want to kill him, his music jives with you, everything is great. Even his hairless chest sprinkled with the odd blond hair here and there gets you even though you're more of a hairy-chest girl. You can't get enough of the smell of his neck; the taste of his lips; the curve of his back. Hell, you even like the snoring that wakes you up at night because it's more time to creepily stare at his unguarded moments, those moments of realness you can sneak in, the moments that have you feeling head over heels.

It's a time to cherish because everything is new. The tattoos on his arms. The way his eyes glance you over from head to toe when he picks you up for a night out, or the way he guides you closer to him with a gentle but firm hand on your back. The way he pulls your shirt when he's feeling cheeky, and the way he strokes your hair. The way he spends an hour going down on you because you're sensitive and hard to please, but he's in it to win it, so he gives it his all.

Everything is new and exciting, and it's the best part!

You're finding yourself sinking deeper and deeper into his quicksand, and you don't want to get out. It's the best part, getting to know him and getting to know the two of you together.

- *Reminder:* To those of us who have started our love adventure with distance woes, the infatuation stage still applies. Think back to when it first started. Did you use Snapchat or Instagram or Facebook more just so your boo could "like" your selfie? Yessss, and don't lie. It was this inexplicable drive you had, this bubble of laughter and excited-ness and expectation that had you calling, texting, emailing, Snapchatting, Instagramming, Facebooking, and in great anticipation to hear from your boo. And when you did, you swooned and showed your girls and talked about it and couldn't *stop* talking about it—the excited new feeling in your chest—and about your boo. That's the infatuation stage. The fun part. So whether you're in person or long distance from the start, it doesn't matter. The feeling is the same.

Chapter 3

Honeymoon Phase:
Let's do Everything Together and Not Get Tired of Each Other Because We Love it!

....

He picks you up after work, takes you on these amazing dates, and suddenly sightseeing the same sights you've seen all your life brings a new breath of fresh air because you're experiencing your city with this man for the first time.

It's all new. All of it. The stupid neon lights. The artificial water show you've seen a million times, the fountains and the lights and the music—and it's all beautiful again. And then he brushes your hair lightly, softly behind your ear, and the fireworks start all over again.

It's an exploration of you. Of him. Of romance. It's hidden in the crevices of you city, the place you grew up in, the one you take for granted. It's hidden in your heavily guarded walls, the ones you put up to protect yourself from everyone and anyone because you've been hurt before. And right there, right then, looking at that beautiful man and his different colored eyes, you realize you've been hiding from all the good too, and his beautiful eyes on you break down all those walls. That moment right then— that's what life is all about.

- *Reminder:* Distance woes. Honeymoon phase. They sound so far apart, because they are. If you're one of the lucky couples who have already visited the other or vise versa (and were not catfished) the first few months of the relationship, good on you! You're one step ahead of the heard, and we all hate you for it.
- If you're not, don't fret! The honeymoon phase is almost always exclusive to being physically together, so when you finally make that trip to your boo or your boo makes that trip to you, you'll have it whether you're new in the relationship or a year out. The honeymoon phase will happen one way or another.

- *Hot Tip:* Let us not forget we live in the twenty-first century in which technology rules our lives. Said technology gives us so much good and so much bad. It can be great for communicating with your boo in Tokyo, and Skyping him too. But it can also be a scary place where people can pretend to be anyone they want, anything they choose to be. It is extremely and urgently advised that if you're traveling to meet your boo, do a simple Skype call or any form of video call. We have so many advantages that with the same technology used to catfish we have at our disposal in verifying identities. This is an issue not of trust, but of self preservation. Be open, fall in love, experience new things—but also be smart, be mindful and always think of your safety first.

Chapter 4

So Now You Know He's Leaving

....

It's been a couple of months, and then he tells you some news you feared, but hoped wouldn't come to be. He has a son, you know this. He's in Montana, you know this too. But now his ex has married and her husband wants to adopt the little boy. The very one that looks every bit like the man sitting in front of you with tears in his eyes and confusion in his heart.

He tells you all these things, you take them in, or you think you do. His mouth is moving and your heart is beating but you're not really feeling anything and you're certainly not comprehending anything. The only thing you know is: there's no way you want to let him go.

I mean, remember how long he stayed down there until the deed was done? You just can't find that kind of devotion anymore, and besides he's not planning on going anywhere, anyway. Not soon, right? Courts take forever and it may even be a few years before he really has to go up there and fight the legal fight. Hopefully not until he's put a ring on your pretty little finger and any chance of escaping your grip is so long gone he'll never even know what happened. He'll choose you.

You entertain yourself with memories of all of his downtown sessions. But then reality sets in and this devoted dad you've put your time and effort into has decided to leave and make things right. Life sucks, and you realize this.

If it was his career he contemplated going back to you would feel the same, you just know it because if it was you making the decision to move away for a career move you know what the answer would be. But it's not you with the quandary that can ruin your life. It's him. And he has his choice to make. And he does, but you can't let him go.

- ◆ *Reminder*: Whether you met your boo while on vacation or he's lived in the town you met for two years, but when you two meet he decides to leave two months into the relationship, making that decision to leave is hard no matter what. Deciding on a career move is more important than your budding romance is hard, but focusing on the future is necessary. Change is never easy, and it won't be for you or your boo. So, if this is your boat, read on.

- ◆ *Hot Tip*: So if your boo (or you) decides to move, be supportive. Talk it out and if keeping the relationship on a long distance level is important to both, try it out. Who knows where this new adventure will take you. Maybe it'll last two more months, or maybe a lifetime. In the end, if it works out and you've stuck it out and two years later your boo is a big shot lawyer in Washington D.C., bitch, you're set. So, in other words, be smart about it.

Chapter 5

So Now He Knows He's Leaving
But He's Still Pursuing You Because You're a Bonafide Goddess and He Knows it

....

He's come to terms with the dreaded news you wish he would take back. After all, you did just laugh at your friend's face when she mentioned her LDR from a few years back.

Remember that tall baseball player who had to travel a lot? Yeah, she didn't just sleep with him every time he was in town. She actually kept a relationship with him well hidden from her besties. Who could blame her? A baseball player in a semi-professional team with a travel itinerary as long as his legs. It wouldn't, it couldn't be anything serious.

So why do it? Why have a long distance thing with someone who could be replaced by many someones as good—or even better—in bed than the one that left? Because when it hits, it hits. Anyone who's ever been in love can attest as to how shitty it can be to fall in love with the wrong person; the short person; the one that makes less money than you; the one with the cute lisp who your friends can't stop making fun of; the one with the short leg; the one who called your friend Lanie instead of Amy and now everyone can't stop talking about something that happened four years ago with a guy that lasted two months!

Love is difficult and hard and when it hits, it hits and you don't care if he's got two teeth and a wart, you love him. Make no mistake, your friends will make fun of him and the distance he's chosen to put between you two because they will make fun of everyone. And anything that adds fuel to the fire is gold. I would do it, you would do it, so stop saying my friends are assholes and secretly patting yourself on the back for your good choices in life.

Just go back and watch Friends on Netflix. Go on, put it on, you know you want to. Season one, episode three. The one with Monica and her new boyfriend she's afraid to introduce to her posse because she knows they'll rip him to pieces. Have you refreshed your memory? Watched the episode? Great, now see what I mean? They all ended up loving the guy, but that's a rare unicorn if there ever was one.

So, this two bit guy, the one with the marvel tongue, says he's come to terms with his heart and his son is just so damn important, and you're left with a pit in your stomach and a sincere desire to go out with your friends on a night of debauchery and dicks. Maybe go to Thunder from Down Under because who the hell does he think he is? That's why. You can get you a real man here, in China or in Mars because you're a fucking boss.

And yet.

He's leaving and you're left devastated. But he won't stop calling, texting, wanting to hang out and making the most of his time left in town. And you give in because—that tongue, for starters—but also those long conversations in the dark, and the way your heart beats when he walks by or breathes or his little pinky moves.

You're fucked, and you know it.

Chapter 6

When It's Over And The Crying Emoji Becomes Your Best Friend

....

He's left. He's gone. You got that final phone call while he was at the airport because you refused to drive him there and cry and make a spectacle so you made his friends drive him there and cry and hug and make a spectacle—but not you. It was your final act of rebellion.

But he's gone, forreal this time.

That deep voice, those different colored eyes, that smile, that tongue—all of it. It's all gone.

It's been a whirlwind of emotions and they've ranged from infatuation to downright anger, but now he's gone and you're feeling the emptiness in the pit of your stomach. The deep hole that's aching and you don't know why you even want to fill it back, like a blackhead after a facial. Empty. Dark. Alone. Lonely.

You wait for it to normalize, but it takes time. It takes baths and wine, and books and music, and pedicures and poolside cocktails. And friends who understand.

You refuse to give in to loneliness and depression so you go out. You make an effort to get pretty, do your hair. Do things that make you happy and make you feel better. You talk about it because what else occupies your mind? How unfair is it, that the only man to oil your rusty gears in the past few months has left for his own damn faults and problems and responsibilities? Why couldn't you just fall for the guy with five children he doesn't worry about? The kind that gets calls from all his baby mommas angrily asking for child support he's behind on. The kind of man who goes around greedily living life like a fucking hedonist without a care in the world except what his lower brain says.

You could get head for hours on end with a guy with no goals, no cares, no worries.

And then your sister slaps you upside the head and reminds you that a goddess like you doesn't go for lowlife guys like that. You may use all the sad emojis you can find, and you will, but you'll get your head back on your shoulders and keep on keeping on.

Because it's what survivors do.

Survive.

♦ *Reminder:* If you started your relationship on a long distance basis, then fuck you very much! You're way ahead of the pack who had to meet, fall for it, and then separate. Pat yourself on the back for a job well done. You weren't catfished, you're not heartbroken, and he's visiting next weekend. So, great. Good. For. You. Skank.

Chapter 7

Wanting To Kill Him is Totally Normal Because He Has a Job and a Son to Get Back to and The Fairytale Ends

....

Once the sadness dissipates, anger sets in. But it's a different kind of anger. It's a deep-rooted anger that is born within you, deeper than any anger you've experienced before because it's the kind of anger that makes you reevaluate your life, your choices, your weaknesses. The kind of anger that says, enough! No more miss nice girl. From now on every guy you're with is fucked. Every. Single. One. Of. Them.

You'll get over it. You will.

So your fairytale ended, so what? So you got a little angry, so what? So you're over it (mostly), and have seen the faults in your reasoning. And now you're back on track. But you still want to kill him for leaving you alone in a cruel, cruel world. Besides, he still hasn't called begging for your attention like he used to. And you'll be dammed if you're the first one to call or text. Fuck that lowlife asshole. Who does he think he is? Playing you like that to see if you break first. He's in for a rude awakening if he thinks you'll break. You're made of steel, motherfucker. You're good. So you're still a little bit angry, so what?

Then the phone rings. It couldn't be a text, could it? He couldn't give you time to think about it, mull your brain over and consult your besties with screenshots of your conversation, could he? He calls, and you're a deer in headlights.

He surprises you again. He misses you. *Well, duh.* He can't stop thinking about you. It's been two months, a week and three days since he left, and he's thought about you every single day. He regrets his decision, but he can't, not really. He's in an uphill battle to the death (or the custody of his child, but still). He's tired, he's lonely, and he's missing you. Montana is different than Vegas. No, he's not interested in meeting girls. He's there with one purpose and one only: for his son. Everything else he has to put up with. He's not whining, he's just being honest.

He's different yet the same. More open. The past two months have made him see things differently. He's sharing. He's including you into his less than perfect life, and he's asking you to be a part of it.

♦ *Reminder:* Sometimes life will throw you a curve ball and you just have to take it, evaluate it, appraise it for the value in your life and keep going. So if he's left and you're missing him and two months later he calls again, trust your gut. If you're still angry and want to make him suffer, then so be it. If you find yourself with a soft heart and a second chance to give, then so be it. You create your life by the choices you make. Don't make a mistake by pushing him out of your life because circumstances happened that took him away (like a job or a son). Chances are he's had to make a tough choice as well, and he's reaching out for what he wants too, hard as it may be to do it.

- *Hot Tip*: On the flip side, don't take him back just because you're lonely. A long distance relationship takes courage, time, effort and so much love. That kind of commitment and time cannot be sustained by mere loneliness and it'll surely end up being a huge waste of time. If you find yourself feeling lonely and wanting to keep the channels of communication open with the one that got away, you can always be friends. That way you'll be free to meet people to fill that void and so will he. In the end, whatever happens will happen but you won't be stopping yourself from getting out there and meeting someone new.

- *Quick Tip*: There's no rule that says you can't get freaky with your best friend, either. So if you want to get weird, by all means. No one has ever said you can't date your friend (long distance or no). So if keeping the lines of communication open is important to you, keep them open! Nothing is stopping you from sending texts updating him with your life or sending him cute selfies on Snapchat.

Chapter 8

Cupid Struck, Now What?

....

It's not enough that he's already called expressing his immense regret, loneliness and undying love for you.

But of course, why wouldn't he feel regret? He's left a perfectly imperfect and funny, smart, fun, gorgeous girl (because sometimes you have to hoot your own horn) behind in a town of duds, fuckboys, and tourists.

You want him to suffer just as you've suffered with his news and his inevitable decision to leave you (for a valuable reason, but still). It's not enough that he's been calling and texting without missing a beat. That he's trying to get in your good senses, that he's just being friendly, because what else can he do? Come over for a midnight boogie? Don't think so. Unless that super fast train was built from Vegas to Montana overnight, but nooo. So he's just being a friend, and so are you.

He has roommates he's close to hating, and he can't wait until his new apartment is ready to move in. He's found a job—not the best, it's not even glamorous, but it pays the bills. Besides, he's there for a little while, just until he resolves his problem, and then he's outta that podunk town with no Best Buy.

When you're not on the phone with him—or texting him, or laughing at his text, or checking your phone for his next quip—you're hanging with your friends, the ones that make fun of your situation.

Cupid struck, boo, and it struck bad.

It's not worth it, they say. What, are you going to have a relationship with your phone? Or are you going to meet flesh and bone guys around town? So you give in. You're just friends with the one that left, anyway. So why not meet people? Live a little.

So you do. You go out with your girls, the skanky ones, the ones that like to party till the sun comes up. You meet guys at bars, nightclubs, midnight shows, venue openings—the works. You drink with them, smile on cue, laugh at their lame jokes—you even give them your number when they ask for it. They text you the next day telling you how much fun they had, how beautiful you are, how amazing you are. But when it comes time to text them back, you can't.

You can't because your heart is somewhere in the middle of fucking Montana.

Chapter 9

Can't Say Hasta La Vista, Baby

....

It's been a while since you two have been hitting the sheets—I mean not *that*, the phone—a while since you two have been hitting the phone. Hard. You two have been talking and texting and Snapchatting and Instagramming and Facebooking, and even Skyping. You do it all and if you were in a relationship you would've taken it to the next level: kinky sex.

But you're not.

You're more than friends but less than partners. You're long distance wannabe's who can't seem to say the right words for fear of sounding like a total douche to the one that just wants to keep it simple, keep it fun, keep it interesting. But at the same time one of you (you) want to take it to the next level, but can't seem to know how to word it.

How do you bring it up, how do you tell him you'd much rather throw him on your bed and have your way with him than go around it? How do you tell him you want to slobber on his anaconda while he pulls your hair and moans and groans your name? You couldn't do it, so you didn't.

Instead, you waited for him to do it. You two were spending a lot of time on each other as it was. What's a little title anyway? Throw in a little exclusivity even if you weren't actually doing the nasty, and bam! You got yourself a long distance thing.

But still.

Have you ever had one of those days when all you want to do is nasty stuff? Like it's the day after your period (or before, or during, or ten days out), and all you want to do is literally be thrown around all day long with a dick in your mouth or your hand or your cooch or all of them at once?

Well, that's how you felt when it started. You wanted to get dirty and nasty and he wanted to keep having deep conversations about your respective childhoods. He thought if he showed you how serious he was about this, how flexible he could be, you would get how much he wanted to be with you—even from a distance—and obviously more than just physically. So you go along with it. Once you even used your trusty pink vibrator while on the phone with him. He was saying something about his dog Chance, and you just said "Uh-huh," or "Oh, yeah," and he didn't catch on. Finally he asked you what the sound in the background was and you lied and told him it was your fan.

He still thinks it was your fan to this day.

What I'm trying to say is long distance relationships will be hard, not just physically, but mentally and emotionally. Some days you'll want dick all day long and won't be able to get it until a month from then, and you'll have to survive it or go to the sex store and get ten vibrators. Sometimes you'll want to wring his neck and you'll have to wait until he visits next and by then it'll be blown over and all you'll want to do is hug him because you miss him already. It'll be hard as hell, but nonetheless, someone has to make the first move, and if it's not going to be you, and it's not going to be him, then just forget it.

You got lucky and he asked you to be in it even from a distance first in a super awkward and painful manner that you still laugh at these days, but when it wasn't happening, it sort of bummed you out. Had he taken a day longer to ask you to make a huge sacrifice and make him exclusive, you would've asked him because what the hell are you doing spending so much time on him if it's not going to pay off, right?

- *Hot Tip*: If your boo is not making the first move, plan on making it yourself. Not the first time you had to take matters into your own hands, is it? What's the harm in one more. If the conversation is flowing and the communication blooming, what's the end point? Wasting your time away on a "friend" who lives a thousand miles away who you talk to on the phone everyday? I don't fucking think so. Take the plunge and do it yourself since your boo's balls obviously haven't dropped yet. Bring it up, and make it clear you want exclusivity if you're going to devote so much time and effort into him. Do it, and watch his mouth drop out of his face because you had more *cojones* than him. You're welcome.

- *Reminder*: Keep in mind it is a huge request, and obviously the persons involved have to have an immense amount of interest in the other to even consider it, so if you're so deep in love you're fucked, you're fucked. And if you're fucked, then go for it. Lord knows who you'd rather spend your time with, even if it is by phone. Fuckboys and duds surround every corner of the world, so when you find The One, stick with him.

Chapter 10

Make Sure it's Worth the Time and Effort Because Sometimes It's Just a Night in Rodanthe

································

It's been established. You're boo, and boo. Bae, and bae. Lovers (over the phone, but still), boyfriend and girlfriend, besties. The whole bit. You call him after anything remotely interesting happens in your life, and he does the same. You can't get enough. It annoys the fuck out of anyone around you, and you relish it. He's it. He may be far, far away, but he holds the proverbial key to your heart, and your cooch.

But what if that's it? Imagine if it would've been just one night in Rodanthe instead of multiple Nights in Rodanthe, and Diane Lane's character had never gotten to know Richard Gere's character. We wouldn't have a tear-inducing movie about long distance love, would we? Nooo. I don't think so.

What if it had been all for naught? What if those letters were full fluff and empty promises, and all he wanted to know is what she would do if he was there? *What that mouf do?* What if he included dick picks along with those letters?

Don't kid yourself, either. A fuckboy will always be a fuckboy.

So, if it's just about sex and the nasty, you have some work to do. Look within you, really deep, and evaluate yourself, your morals, and what you want in a relationship. Don't give a fuckboy the time of day, and certainly don't waste those minutes on a guy who's not even worth a donut hole from the donut shop down the street. It's deceiving in the way that it's going to be good the minute you put it in your mouth. The sweet decadence, the soft, round shape overtaking your mouth, the chewiness surrounded by just the right amount of crunchiness—and then it's over. You want to go back for more, but you know you can have twenty of those little suckers, and it wouldn't mean anything. It will never be a donut. Never. Ever.

Make sure he's worth your time, effort, and love, because a long distance relationship takes time, patience, unconditional love, and immense trust. A donut hole can pretend to be a donut all it wants, but it will never deliver. Keep that in mind.

The flip side of a fuckboy is an honest man. A loving man. A respectable man. A man who you can see yourself with, loving with, building a life with, a family with. If you can't see that, then what's the point? What's the end game? Sure, some relationships are casual, but it's stated as so, and not to be taken seriously—and more importantly, not to be had long-distance. If all you want is a casual thing, and all he's willing to give is a casual picture showing you his D, forget it. It won't last and it will be a colossus waste of time for both parties involved. Besides, you can get that in your own town with real guys who have time and the undeniable desire to give you those downtown sessions you so miss.

- *Reminder*: Don't become suspicious about every little thing either, because that can turn into another kind of nightmare for you. If he's feeling friskier than usual, let him be! You get your days where nothing can sate you, right? Well, so does he. Learn to trust yourself, your intuition, your gut. If you can trust the guy, then go for it. If there's a nagging deep within you telling you to run the other way, follow your gut. It's smarter than the heart. In so many ways.

◆   *Hot Tip*: Not all relationships are serious. You get that. But if a long distance relationship is not serious, then you're wasting your time, girl. Might as well go out on a wild night out and find a guy to have fun with for the time being, because your long distance love is probably doing the same. Not to make you paranoid or anything, but rules have to be made and kept, by both, 100% of the time. At least, that's my rule. And if he feels like straying, all he has to do is say so.

◆   *Author's note*: I once ended a casual relationship because I decided to date another man (who turned out to be the worst decision of my life, but I learned, didn't I?). If another person is catching my attention more than you, or I'm wondering what else is out there, forget it. The same applies to him, he has free will to let me know when and if he's been tugged another way. All you have to do is speak up!

Chapter 11

When it Becomes
a Long Distance Relationship and How to Handle the Truth
of Your Life and Decisions

....

You've made some good decisions in your life, and some not so good. Now you're texting your boo more than ever, planning your day for that nightly call, and on occasion wearing sexy lingerie that you're just going to take off yourself before flopping into bed after hitting send. You find yourself hoping that sexy selfie can withstand a week without another request because you feel like recycling lingerie is lame, and giving all that effort to look sexy for nothing is weighing you down.

It's hard being sexy for your phone, and it's even harder when you have to imagine all the possible scenarios instead of living them, but still. You digress.

He's the one, and you'll do whatever it takes to keep him, because he's also sent you that morning selfie with that bedhead you love so much, the one with the cheeky grin and the five-o'clock shadow that hits the spot just right. You can't give him up now if you tried. It would take a village and your parents threatening to keep you out of their will if you don't stop that nonsense, and even still, you'd think about it.

It's a give and take, and it seems to be working for now. But sometimes the reality of your situation hits you hard. I mean, *hard*. It'll come at unsuspecting moments, like when you're trying on that pair of shoes you're never going to get because they're five hundred dollars over your budget, and you're all like *yassss, get it hunty*, but then your bank account balance flashes in your brain, and the magic is done—and it's at this very moment the universe aligns, and the couple walking hand in hand, all smiles, and red roses blooming around them, and love hanging around them like little demons will hit you right smack in the face like a ton of chocolate covered strawberries, and leave you with such a fucking deep hole in your stomach, that not even a call from your boo would do at this moment.

It's at this moment you choose to evaluate your life choices and the path they've taken you down. A lonely, lonely path. And you think it wasn't that long ago that was you walking hand in hand with your man, all smiles and glee. It was just a few bad decisions, more than a few braincells, and a cupid's arrow ago. And oh, how good it looks to go back. You just wanna go back.

Then, as if on cue, your brain rewires, and reminds you of all those duds you've dated, all those pricks with dick pics, all those half-hearted sentiments you've heard just to get in your pants, all those nights with a man by your side, hand in hand, yet still not feeling as full and fulfilled as you do now with your boo miles away, and your heart is in your throat because that man, handsome and awesome as he may be, is still an asshole for making you go through this, and even more so for living so far, far away.

◆ *Reminder*: Make a decision and stick with it. You've been fickle all your life, I know. You've swayed from idea to idea, college to college, town to town, boy to boy. I know. It's still early. You still have time to run, run away and never look back if you want to. So, if you have it in you to do it, do it. If you can't imagine losing him and what you have, far as he may be, stick with it. Know the road ahead is long, and hard, and full of hardships and troubles, but the results will also be full of love, laughter, and getting to know yourself and him in ways you never knew. Distance makes you more honest, more loving, more accepting, more...*more*. Everything is heightened, adored, revered, and appreciated. Because when it's worth it, it's hard. But oh, so rewarding.

Chapter 12

Setting the Tone and Living the Rules

....

If it hasn't become clear enough, you're living in a shell only you can feel, and no one can see. It's difficult sometimes to explain to those who love you why you do the things you do, but in the end it's not up to them. It's up to you and your well thought out decisions. After all, it's your boat he's rocking, your ear he's talking off at night when both of you have time to sneak away from your busy lives.

Even at times when a relationship is so well off—distance be dammed—setting the tone, and grounding some rules is a must.

When The One and you met, it was all sparkles and cotton candy skies. When he left the tone changed. You were at a point where relationships build into something stronger, something thicker. It wasn't just physical, and it wasn't infatuation. It was getting real, meaty.

The big move changed a lot. It thickened the plot, so to speak. It could've been the end, but it wasn't. It was just the beginning. Being so far from each other created other, more difficult troubles than what you imagined. It wasn't, "no you come over after work because I went over last time." It wasn't, "come with me to my parents 30th anniversary and skip that office party you've been looking forward to because I'm more important than you and your job put together." Those kind of problems didn't exist.

It was more along the lines of: "What did you do today?" "Oh, really?" "Hmmm..." "Was she cute?" "I don't care if she just cut your hair, I want to know if she's cute!"

It also went this way: "Oh you're hanging out with your friend, nice." "Oh, it's a guy??" "Well, he better not try anything or I'll kick his skinny ass from here to Peru." "Oh, you've known him for ten years and he's never tried anything with you?" "That's not even possible. Guys and girls just cannot be friends without an alternate motive. It just is."

Jealousy. That's the bottom line. Most other problems are inconsequential, because what it boils down to is unabashed, ugly, sneering, crippling jealousy. It stands to reason jealousy will peek it's snaky head in any relationship, but for a long distance relationship, you can magnify it by a thousand and then some.

Jealousy can be many things. It can be jealousy of your work and the time you devote to it, it can be jealousy of your neighbors and the space you share with them, jealousy of friends and the time you spend with them, or it can be jealousy of the opposite sex and the possibility of infidelity. Jealousy comes in many shapes and sizes, and not one of them is healthy.

So, to avoid some unpleasant situations, setting some ground rules is imperative. Figure out what your biggest obstacles are, the biggest hurdles you have to overcome and set rules to offset them.

For instance, if his biggest problem is jealousy regarding your friends and the time you spend with them—especially those of the male species—he'll want to (but certainly won't) set a rule stating that when you go out with your guy friends you have to text him the minute you leave and every fifteen minutes thereafter to satisfy his caprice that you aren't getting into some unknown unmentionables or vise versa.

Your immediate response will be the correct one: to laugh your ass off. No man can, and certainly no man will tell you what you can and can't do. You can certainly tell him what to do, because duh, but no no no no no, no way.

What you'll eventually come up with is a *rule*. You can choose to tell him when you're going out with your guy friends and he can choose to fret, or you can choose to tell him when you're going out with your guy friends and he can choose to trust that your cooch will stay well protected by your granny panties and your thick pair of jeans. If not, then he would just have to trust your silky red pair of panties will stay on all night, and the only thing going in your mouth is the Jean Philippe Dulce de Leche crepe you'd been dying for.

The rule? Telling him you're hanging out with your dangerous biker friends. It's all about inclusion, you see. The bigger rule? He has to trust you. Plain and simple.

Then there are *your* rules: No eye contact with any other girl. No talking to women. Period. No checking anyone else out; no liking selfies on Facebook, Instagram; no Snapchatting with skanks; no thinking of any other women except you and you alone. No talking to women cashiers, no getting his hair cut by women, no nothing that involves women. Porn has to go too. What does he have to look at naked beautiful girls with beautiful bodies that can contort in any compromising position when he could simply think of you?

You'll want to set those rules, but if control is what you want, get a seven speed vibrator. You'll have better luck controlling the speeds on that monster. Jealousy ≠ trust. And trust ≠ jealousy. You can't have both, only one or the other.

Other couples will be totally okay with having an open relationship in between visits, and if that works for you and your boo, talk it out and decide on the rules for your relationship. What may work for some may not work for others. Maybe going on dates is okay, but not sex with another person. Maybe casual sex is okay, but no dates. Figure out the tone of your relationship and apply rules that fit with both parties.

- ◆ *Hot Tip*: You can't control what another person chooses to do, but you can control what you do, so if you're in a relationship that is based on jealousy and distrust, dig deep and figure out if it's worth keeping. Some relationships can get violent, even from a distance, and fear and violence are never okay. If you have trouble figuring out what kind of relationship you have, write a pro/con list, talk to your friends, voice the problems and if it's too far gone, or on a whole different level, you're at a safe distance to call it quits! Block his number, block him on all social media, and keep busy, because it can be so hard to stay committed to your decision, but also so necessary to let it go if it's not safe, or what you really want.

- ◆ *Quick Tip*: It can be so easy to give in, to think you love him so much it's all worth it. That all of his requests (or demands) are okay. And no, I'm here to tell you it's not okay. He's not making requests from a place of harmony, it's quite the opposite. So be strong, and remember that you are a goddess who deserves all the good she wants. Nobody wants to end up like Jennifer Hyatte who broke her bae out of prison and killed a guard in the process. All she had to say was no, dude. No way. I'm here in the free world, and you're stuck in there for some crime you committed, so wait it out, man. No harm no foul. Now she's rotting in jail for some two-bit criminal who got in her head. Not worth it.

Chapter 13

Peeing and the Importance of Being Earnest

....

You've established some ground rules (which are pretty much all DO NOT CHEAT ON ME OR ELSE), you've talked it out, let yourself be vulnerable by showing your fears, wants, and expectations.

Now it's time to be honest.

Honesty and candor do a relationship good, trust me. I'm not talking about the run of the mill honesty. You know what I'm talking about. The real, sometimes dirty, occasionally gross, and always vulnerable honesty. It happens without a second thought sometimes, and it's hard to stop. And really, you shouldn't.

It may come in any form or way, maybe you told him your deep, dark, nerdy secret that you loved Twilight, and fell deeply in love with a sparkly vampire (or maybe the wolf suited your caprice better), whatever it may be, everything you want to hide will come out whether you want it to or not. So might as well just give in, let him in, pour your soul. Because while you're opening up, so is he. And the results will be so much more.

So, how did you let him in? Well, here you go. After a few months of nightly talking on the phone with your boo (texting alone wasn't and isn't going to cut it), you got so comfortable with each other that it wasn't anything new when you stopped muting the phone while you went tinkle, and after a few giggles and *I can't believe I just did that*, and *I can't believe you just did that,* the mood changed, you became closer in a deeper way than just a "long distance relationship." It brought you two closer together, to share something so intimate, yet so a part of relationships everywhere.

Soon after he felt comfortable enough to do the same with you, and the next time you muted the phone while you tinkled he asked you why you did so. You said to have some privacy and to spare him, but he wouldn't have it. You've peed with him on the phone ever since. The next time he muted the phone you asked him why, he said the same, privacy, spare me, blah blah blah. You told him not to, and he hasn't. It's kind of weird to admit, but you like hearing him in that human act.

You feel closer to him.

Once he said he had to call you back in five minutes, so you let him go. When he called back, you had a series of questions for him: why did you have to hang up (at this point you were even cooking while on the phone), what was so important, and so secret you had to hang up? The answer: it was number two. Sometimes it's good to hang up, sometimes, it's good to ask questions, sometimes it's not. You've never questioned his five minute breaks again. It's a learning experience.

Don't get me wrong, a certain level of privacy and allure is lost when you start peeing while on the phone—not to mention mystery—the echo of the bathroom walls an unmistakeable giveaway. The alternative to that situation would be the in-person equivalent to that stage in your relationship, where you feel comfortable enough to pee in front of your boo.

Maybe it would be after he gives you a foot massage, and your bladder had been pushing against you for the past half hour but you didn't want him to stop, and you can't hold it any longer so you run to the bathroom but he's telling you a super important story so he follows along so you don't miss it, and before you know it bam! You've peed in front of him, and you laugh when you realize it, and he laughs and that's that.

The next time it happens you're brushing your teeth, and he's late for work, and he barges in and takes care of business and you remind him to stop by your favorite Thai place for that curry you've been dying for because you already know you won't have time to do so, and he agrees and kisses your cheek while moving you out of the way so he can wash his hands and he's gone before you know it, and bam! It's done. No biggie. Just a part of a strong and healthy relationship.

You could map it out, you could put it on a grid and calculate the exact moment it would've happened if he was here, in person, but he's not, and you're not. You don't have to map it all out, it will just happen that way, the way most things happen. It feels right, so don't stop it, don't prevent it, just go with the flow. So, no, don't map it, don't make it mechanical (unless you're stubborn as hell, in which case I can't stop you and you're going to do it anyway so go ahead, map it), just let things happen. It's the best to just. Let. Things. Happen. You'll be much happier, and free for it.

- *Reminder*: No, it does not mean you're into kinky crap if you pee while on the phone. It simply means you've crossed another threshold, another step, another level. It's pretty much the opposite of kinky. It's normal! It's just another thing you do.

- *Reminder Deux*: If you are into kinky crap, good for you! More power to you, no one is here to judge you, but the rest of us remain unmoved. It's not kinky, it's normal!

Chapter 14

The Blooming Romance

....

You've peed on the phone, you've expressed your fears and wants, and now, it's going steady and nice, like a river bank you like swimming in, calm yet satisfying. It's moving, but it's so smooth and wonderful, and you enjoy the calmness of it all. You can count on his phone call at exactly the same time every night, except those days when he works twelve hours instead of eight, and you know when he's showered in the mornings because he's texted you, *"Good morning, beautiful. Jumping in the shower now and wishing you were here ;),"* without fail. He calls you during his lunch, and even on his breaks, and when you don't answer he leaves you the cutest messages you go back to listen to over and over when you need to hear his voice.

You text him while you're at work about your pesky co-worker who keeps stealing your Cheeze-it box when you need it the most, and you send him a series of texts when your newborn nephew poops on you while changing his diaper. It's a steady stream of sharing, laughing, enjoying, loving. It's the perfect time to be and you just want to wrap yourself in a comfy blanket of your love and his love and make babies with it so that you can wrap those blankets on you too.

This is the bliss phase.

It will pass.

It's not until you get mad at him for something silly, like forgetting to text you good night, even though he's said it over the phone that you get to know the real you, and the real relationship you have. It's not until he gets mad at you for hanging up on him for laughing about your Cookie Crisp cereal that you realize just how deep in it you are. So what you're a twenty-something who likes cookies for breakfast? And when you don't pick up his next three calls, you feel smug about it. He's sorry, you just know it. And then he doesn't call the 4th time because he's somewhat prideful so you call and he doesn't pick up and it's a vicious cycle. So when he finally calls back, he says he's sorry, and you do too. And it's back to that river bank of bliss and peacefulness until the next capricious thing happens and then all over again.

Hidden within the waves of caprice is the talk of the future, the conversation that keeps it all moving forward because if all you had were phone calls and texts and cyber fights, then you'd be doomed, but you have one thing to look forward to, and one thing only: The Future.

It's when your relationship has stopped budding, and it's now blooming.

Talk of the house you'll buy when you both live in the same city is always fun, and what's not to like about the Mercedes he insists you drive (along with your byproduct in the back seat), but what gets deep and creates a love so deep is when you talk about mundane things. How fun it will be when he's showering and you flush the toilet ten times just to mess with him, or how he'll make breakfast in bed for you wearing only an apron and bring it on a platter for you and how he'll feed you slowly even though he wants you to hurry so he can make love to you. Or when he finally gets to taste your secret recipe pancakes everyone loves, or when he cooks the curry he's been studying up on just to make it that much more special. Or when you'll finally be able to lay your head on his chest, listening to his heart beating in person, in the flesh. Or when he'll get to feel your legs around him.

Things to look forward to make the world go round.

- *Reminder:* Sharing your life through the phone line, or text, or Snapchat or whatever you prefer is perfectly normal. Some people want to hide things that make them feel vulnerable. I say, show it! Nothing will bring you closer than sharing those little things about you that feel too personal, because they are. So if you like to eat pickles in the middle of the night while you talk to your boo, share that with him. Chances are he'll have a jar of your favorite kind in his place when you visit and then you'll really know he's listening and he cares.

- *Hot Tip*: Make the world go round by talking about the future. It's not a plan yet, it's just fun, but fun that will get things moving. The more you daydream, the more you desire. For those of us in long distance relationships, daydreams get us through the rough days, so do it, and do it often.

Chapter 15

He's Already Cried on the Phone so Obviously You're Close Now

....

Emotions happen to us all.

Let me say that again.

Emotions happen to us all.

Say it over as many times as you need, because it doesn't matter how manly your memory of him was, the closer you get, the deeper he feels, the more he opens up to you, and don't mistake it.

You're the one he's chosen to open up to. How many women do you think he'd cry in front of (or on the phone or FaceTime)? I'd go on a limb and say after his mother and sisters, not many. Especially if he's from a little town in Montana where crying is frowned upon and lifted trucks and guns are praised.

Soul search if you must, but once he cries on the phone, you're close.

Let that sink in.

Go ahead and mute the phone while you laugh and wonder what the hell you're doing with your life that it's brought you to this moment of fucking evil despair. When you want to laugh at the emotions of your boo, when the crying is so real, but so is the fucking feeling in the pit of your stomach that won't let you breathe properly until you have a big, good laugh. So have it, laugh to your hearts content, and then calm down, take deep breaths, because now that he's opened up so deep, and so fully all that's left is for you to support him. Guide him. Trust him. Build him up. That's what he's really asking you to do.

Maybe it happens on a particularly bad day at work, or after a bad court meeting. Maybe it happens after he hangs out with his neighbor (who's turned into his best friend since the big move), his wife and adorable kids, and he has the feels because you're so far away. Maybe it's after he had a dream of you leaving him, or choosing someone else, or kissing a frog who turns into a prince, or whatever. He still has these fears, because he's so far away, and he doesn't know how to control them because they're as new to him as this whole thing is to you and he can't stop them. That ugly fear you have, he has. That nasty worry you have, he has. That dream you look forward to, he looks forward to. Any desire you have, he has. So, be there for him. Comfort, guide, trust, because that's what he's asking you for. He just doesn't know how.

♦   *Reminder*: It's so hard for (some) men to ask for comfort. It just is. So they show it in different ways, let it out in different manners. Maybe he's complaining about something, jump in there and comfort him. Call him cute names, give him nicknames. Have at least five nicknames for your boo for different moods you're in. It makes him feel special and wanted. If you answer the phone with, "What's up, dude?" and he shows an aversion to the casualness of it, call him baby, or the Henry to your Anais, or Tyrone—whatever works for you. He'll be back to normal once he feels that your feelings for him are just the same as they were last night when you were buttering him up after a sexy FaceTime session. It's simple, the comfort he seeks. It's your warmth from afar. So say it, say it all the time, and then again. The benefits will be worth the cheesiness.

Chapter 16

How Long is Too Long Without Seeing Each Other?

....

Months can go by without any physical contact in a long distance relationship. That's what you signed up for when you decided to keep going after he left. It's that simple.

So, how long is too long without a visit? It all really depends on what job you hold, the distance in between, finances, and the free time to travel. If you have a particularly shitty boss who won't let you take two days off to fly to Montana, get picked up by bae, walk around the tiny "downtown" until you can't hold it in any longer and downright ask him to get you home and fuck you before you lose it (fuck your romantic dinner, asshole, you left me four moths ago!), and still have time to romantically wake up with your head on his chest, have a little quickie before breakfast and spend the next day like a decent adult with a little R&R, then you're fucked. Because that's exactly what can happen, and often times, it will.

Let's be honest, it sucks. There's no such thing as "free time" to travel and there never will be.

It's been close to five months since your boo left, and five months since you've seen him. He's started a new job, and missing even a day of work is hard for him (especially as a new hire), and though he's just a couple of hours away by plane, you feel farther away because of the vastly different lives you lead, and all the space in between. It's not just your job or his job, you see, it's planning around birthdays and work dinners, and your friend's baby shower (snobby bitch) or bachelorette party (lucky bitch), or trying for that three day weekend that you both will have off three months from now even though it seems like forever away.

It's hard work. It's difficult to include a long distance beau in your every day life. But with enough will, and plenty of desire (hello, hormones), it's doable.

It will *never* be the right time, and you will never have free time. You will always have a dinner to go to, a friend who needs your advice after breaking up with her douchebag boyfriend (who is nothing like yours), or a family members' friends' cousins' best friend's birthday party your presence is required at. But sometimes, you have to put your needs ahead of other's needs.

Inclusion is the best form of flattery, and also a real solution to a pesky problem. Want to show him off? Bring him to your great grandmother's 90th birthday party. Want to make him feel included? Have him over for that weekend you know your second cousins from New York are coming for the week. Want to overwhelm him? Tell him it's okay if he comes over for a quick weekend when your parents have scheduled a fancy dinner. He'll feel much more included, and the meet the parents kind of thing would've happened if you were together (in person) anyway. So just go out on a limb and do it! Have him come over when it's your nephew's first birthday party. It'll be cute, and he'll get to meet the whole family, and make his presence known.

It'll be scary for him to walk into a home full of your family, especially if he's never met them before, but it'll be worth it. He'll have a clear picture of who's who in your family and possibly even build a relationship with your dad. Maybe they'll even call each other on the phone on occasion to discuss the importance of fishing in Alaska. Your mom won't be able to wait until he makes the move back permanently, because he made such a splash at the party and everyone loved him (and because, duh, her daughter can't move states away from her so it'll have to be him).

- ◆ *Hot Tip*: If he can't visit you because of job restrictions or lack of time, and you can't go visit because of work restrictions and lack of time, plan a date when you two can travel...halfway. All of a sudden, The Black Eyed Peas' *Can You Meet Me Halfway* is making a lot more sense, isn't it? If spending a weekend away is not possible, plan for a day in a town or city on the halfway mark and get a hotel. There's nothing wrong with spending a day in a hotel making love and ordering room service. Or walking around and sightseeing, whatever floats your boat. At the very least, you'll see each other and know the other is just as invested in it as you are.

- ◆ *Reminder*: Some of us are lucky to live just states away, some of us are lucky if we can get a visit every six months because bae is countries away. Whatever your case, hang in there. Distance sucks the life out of anyone, but it can't suck the love out of anyone, only those that let it.

Chapter 17

When to Travel

....

The best time to travel is whenever you freaking want to, that's when. But if you have a shitty boss (see previous chapter), you have to plan, plan, plan. Planning when to travel can be tricky, but if you have the freedom to give it some time between flights, plan your next one in advance, preferably one (him) and one (her).

What do I mean by that? Well, let me explain. What you're doing is a relationship. Not a oneship—a relationship. Between two people. Two adult people. Two adult people that can travel. Two adult people that *should* travel. Travel should not fall to just one party, not even one party most of the time while the other sits by looking pretty, waiting for the other to arrive. It should be equal. Like most things are nowadays, except equal pay because DO NOT GET ME STARTED. You get the picture.

By planning your flight early (or coordinating with your boo's flight), not only will the tickets be cheaper, but the knowledge that your next romp in the sheets is coming up will be more than enough to keep you entertained. That is, until your actual romp in the sheets, because damn, it's few and far between no matter the frequency.

- ◆ *Hot Tip*: Most airlines vary in price, but one thing that stays pretty consistent is best time for booking. The best time to buy tickets can vary, but according to Cheapair.com[3], who studied over a billion flights, the very best time to book is fifty-four (54) days in advance, with prime booking at 112 to twenty-one (21) days in advance. There were some variables in their study—some flights being cheaper at fifty-three (53) days, some at fifty-two (52), some on the very day the flights went on sale, and some (a tiny fraction) on the last day. So, plan, plan, plan, and you might save on that romp in the sheets, and what's better than that.

- ◆ Cheapair.com has also created a chart for better planning.

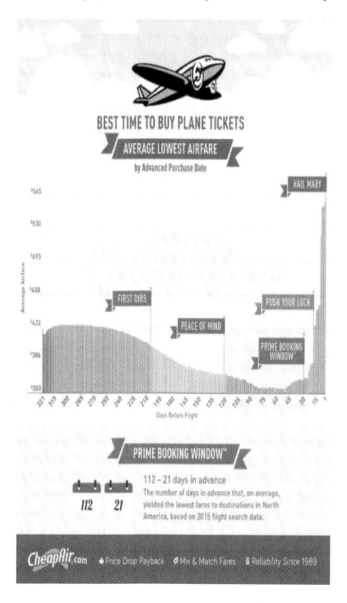

◆   *Quick Tip*: For those traveling Internationally, here's a chart for best booking times.

Cheapair.com/International

Chapter 18

Who Travels First?

....

You hoped this wouldn't come out to the light. You hoped not to ever say this again, or to entertain the thought.

But here it is.

You're petty.

As fuck.

But you're also a girl (or guy), and you have a vagina (or an anaconda). You have the power. You RULE. And in that spirit, you make your boo travel first. And that's that. You will travel to your boo, too, but the first flight will go to your boo. And that's that.

The intention is quite clear. Your boo left you. You didn't want a long distance relationship, but here you are.

You don't want to say you're being petty as shit and punishing him for leaving, but yeah, that pretty much sums it up. If the desire hits, make your boo visit you first, and make him do it with a smile on his face.

After all, the first time you realized you had dominion over your boo is when he FLAT OUT TOLD YOU. I mean, if it was meant to be a secret, why say it? He said you could make him do anything you wanted, and you have—to a certain degree. You don't want a puppet, okay, you just want a very pliable man-toy to do as you please.

Just kidding.

Really.

You want a man who will agree with most of what you say, especially when you're right (which is all the freaking time), and do what you say with a smile on his gorgeous face. That's it. That's all you want. And it's not too much to freaking ask for, thank you very much.

- ◆ *Reminder*: Some of us have different long distance relationships. Some started out as long distance, some had the misfortune of leaving in the middle of something good. Who travels first isn't really a fight to win more than it is who can actually travel first. Maybe you're in a different country and can't get a passport for three more months, but your boo already has one issued and valid. Your boo can travel first. And once your passport is ready, travel to your boo. It's not math, and it's not difficult, but it can always be petty.

- ◆ *Hot Tip*: Steering clear from those petty feelings (like making your boo see you first even though they can't for a while) can be hard. It can be especially hard if you feel like you've been done bad. If your boo left, then it's up to him to make it up, but what if he can't? At least not for the next four months. Getting out of your head and visiting him first is not giving in. If anything, it's an adventure you would've otherwise not taken. Who has the desire to visit a small town in Montana if not to see your boo? Maybe if you're into that kind of stuff, but honestly, small town Montana may not be in everyone's radar. So take the plunge! Go on an adventure, and more importantly, go get what you want.

Chapter 19

Is it Petty to Make Him Work at it?

....

Let me get one thing straight. You are not petty. You're really not. I mean, You will make your man work extra hard for you, and give you gifts, and sing you to sleep even if it's over the phone, and send you not the birthday gift he wanted to send (Brett Favre jersey, eww), but the one you really wanted (Tiffany's gold citrine ring, *sigh*) and let him think it was all his wonderful idea.

You will do that with no regret or worry in your intelligent, pretty head. You will guilt him into visiting you more than you visit him, and make him send you nude selfies before you send your semi nudes, because you can, duh. And you do. You can persuade him to do pretty much anything you want, and you take pride in that.

You know what else you do? You call him every day and leave him the cutest messages when he doesn't answer, you send him texts about you and your life, things you think about, your favorite things about him, your favorite body parts of his you love and miss, and pretty much everything else. You plan the best birthdays for him, you surprise visit anytime you can, and you give him amazing head.

You are loyal, and faithful, and try to be everything for him. You're his ride or die because that's what you want and expect from him too. You want it all. But you also give it your all. You work at it, hard. But you also want to know he's working at it, and not just because you ask him to. You want him to want it. You want him to want *you*.

Wanting to feel wanted is not petty. It's the most normal thing in the world. And if someone is not giving you what you want from them, then something's gotta change, no?

- *Reminder*: You have to housebreak a puppy before he can be the cute ball of fur you like to cuddle with and take selfies with. Men are no different. You have to tell them what you want, and once you tell them, you've got to show them. So take that shy veil off your peppy attitude, because in a long distance relationship, you're definitely going to need it full force.

- *Hot Tip*: Feeling shy? Try breaking out of your shell little by little. Have a request you've been too shy to voice? Take the next hour to take a deep breath, exhale, count to ten, meditate for half an hour, and once you're done connecting to the universe, feel like the goddess you are and call him. Call him and tell him something you've been dying to tell him but you've been too shy to. It can be as simple as, "I want you to visit me more frequently," to "I really like it when we're getting down and dirty and you do that thing you do...I've been thinking about that all day long," and just go for it. Be assertive. Your relationship will thank you later.

Chapter 20

Trust and Other Mythical Feelings

....

There comes a time in every long distance relationship when the issue of trust is going to be brought up more than others. And that time is when you're going out to (INSERT EVENT HERE). It may happen at any given moment.

Oh, your nephew is graduating from Kindergarten? Cute, try telling your boyfriend in Montana you're not going to gobble down any dick while you clap for your munchkin in an adorable mini cap and gown, and take a thousand pictures of the cutie pie.

Oh, it's Thanksgiving and your boo couldn't make it but you've planned out the meal for weeks and now it's the day but your mom invited John from high school (the one that recently got divorced), and your boyfriend in Montana isn't feeling so hot about your old boyfriend sharing a meal of gratefulness with you? Tough luck. You can't avoid the world just because he's not with you. Besides, he's going to pout whether you Skype him or not.

Rules or no rules, trust is a feeling that must be fed. Constantly.

Remember that chapter where we discussed Rules and Setting the Tone? Yeah, that's out the window. It worked for a while, and it still does most of the time, but moments like these, when you're being spread thin, are the moments when your loyalty will truly shine bright, or willow in the depths of his despair.

On the other hand, it may happen to you too. It'll happen when he mentions his cousin twice removed is in town with one of her best friends who just happens to be super hot, and an Instagram model to top it off. They're planning on dinner and drinks, but now you're not feeling so hot and you wish you could jump on the next flight and hold his hand all night long while you whisper sweet nothings in his ear and touch his butt every five minutes and declare him your property because he's yours because he is and because you say so.

Or maybe it'll be when his conveniently single coworker has car troubles and your boo volunteers to drop her off home after work one evening because her apartment is on the way anyway, but all you want to do is scream at the top of your lungs that he's yours and she's a stupid skank with a stupid car and you wished she would just go away and hide in Yellowstone for a year and a half while her leg hair grew into an unmistakeable semblance to Big Foot. And when he asks you where your trust is you say it's probably in Disneyland or where Peter Pan lives because you sure as shit don't feel like trust is real at that moment and that's your story and you're sticking to it.

♦ *Reminder*: There comes a moment when you or your boo will ask for trust—demand it, really—to believe in your love, have faith that the distance is temporary, but the love is not. That one day all of this will be worth it, that someday it won't matter if he's going to a bar with a distant cousin and her pretty friend, or that your long lost high school sweetheart is making his way to your parents house for Thanksgiving because one day you and your boo will walk in to that Thanksgiving dinner hand in hand, and one day he'll be smiling as he looks lovingly at you in that bar with his distant cousin and that Instagram model in tow. That one day, all these mythical feelings will be real, because the distance will be closed by the love you both share. And though that day may also feel mythical, it's real. It is so real.

Chapter 21

What to do During the Interim and How to Deal With Those Pesky Feelings of Doubt

....

The interim.

It's the (sometimes fun) time apart between visits. It is also the devil. Don't get me wrong, I love the interim just as much as the next girl, but consider this: it can go both ways; white or black, left or right, forwards or backwards. It can be a relaxing time, a time to reflect, a time to get to know yourself better, a time to feel free of stigmas and pressures, a time to be yourself without apology, a time to read, laugh, love, smile, cry without shame, tan by the pool, go out and dance, eat in bed, go on that trip with your friends, take bubble baths and drink wine—a time to enjoy everything in life and just *be*.

It can be so fun and freeing. You have all the time of a single person without actually being single. You're never really alone, and you're never really lonely. You still get those calls and texts that you appreciate so much and love so much, and then you get to share what you did that day—it's all beautiful.

It can also be a time of doubt, worry, anxiety, premature conclusions and fear. It's a downward spiral if you let the bad thoughts get in, because one minute you're thinking about his cute face lying on the pillow just like the picture he sent you ten minutes ago, and the next it's wondering if he's really alone or if some skank took the picture just to keep you sated. Then you call him and wake him up even though he has to work extra early the next day, but you spend an hour on the phone while he's trying to convince you he's really alone, he's really in this relationship, and he really loves you.

You risk your sanity, but that's always better than taking the next flight out just to prove your point, and then it comes crashing around you when you realize he's really alone and you're really a psycho.

Or it can be a time when you're going out with your girls, you're dressed to the nines, you got your cute heels on, your lipstick on, and your hair teased and curled. You're enjoying your night out with your girls—something you don't do nearly enough—when your boo calls you and asks you why you haven't texted the past twenty minutes, or answered his last five calls. He tells you he thinks you're with another guy, but you assure him you're not, but he won't have it. Now you're considering having your girls talk to your boo, who is usually cool, but in his current condition you consider shutting off your phone and just enjoy your night, but that would be another never-ending fight, so you let it go.

You ask him to remember that time you called him, your psycho proudly showing, and he assured you he was in it to win it. You're the same, you tell him, just the same. You're going out, but you have him in your heart, your mind, and your soul. Nothing can change that. Not even a night out on the town. It's all true because you'd rather have a quiet night in with your boo than random hookups for the next five months, you'd rather keep him despite the distance, than imagine anyone else in your life, you'd rather fight and claw, and scream and shout. And keep him. And you tell him.

It's the interim.

You can't be a shut-in, and neither can he. So he tells you he loves you, to keep that in mind. And you say you love him too, keep that in mind.

- ◆ *Reminder:* The interim can be fantastic or it can be a can of crap. It is what you make it and nothing else. With constant communication and honest talks, cute selfies and bubble baths, Skype calls and FaceTime at the market, sleeping while on the phone and hearing him snore, sending postcards when you go to the beach and receiving some from Yellowstone, sending cute texts and receiving cheesy voice messages—it's all what you make it even on days when you're out having fun and living life. So make it the best, and trust your gut!

Chapter 22

How to Know When You're Psychotic

....

See "What to do During the Interim and How to Deal With Those Pesky Feelings of Doubt," second paragraph. I'm just saying. You know when you've lost it. And hopefully that's not when you're stabbing your boo with a fork after taking the first flight out just because you're feeling like something's amiss.

I mean, it's all about love and fun and awesomeness until he says something that rubs you the wrong way and then it's all downhill from there. You're seeing red, and no matter what you do, stabbing him with a fork is all you want to do. But you don't, because that would be PSYCHO, and that you're not.

You're much, much worse.

You're *intuitive*.

Chapter 23

How to be Intuitive

....

Intuition can really be simplified down to a quick, easy to understand definition: The act of being psychotic without outwardly showing you're psychotic.

Easy peasy.

I mean, if you're going to listen to that voice in your head telling you your boo is not home like he said and he's most likely balls deep in a skank, you might as well pack for the looney bin. But change "that nagging voice in your head" to "that still small voice that guides you" (um, hello), or say you have an advanced sixth sense, or you've just always trusted your gut, and you're home free. That's what intuition does for you. Makes you legit.

So, the next time you're feeling a little psychotic, a little deranged, a little batshit crazy, use your god-given ability and use your intuition. We all have gut feelings. That's why it's such a cliché! I don't want you to turn into a tie-dye hippy, reefer using, hairy armpit owner, tarot reading gypsy, LSD eating adventurer. I don't. Unless you already are, in which case, more power to you!

Intuition is something we all have. It's as real as the air we breathe, and just as invisible. So the next time you're feeling a little batshit crazy, just say you trust your well built, and rather trustworthy intuition. Especially when in the midst of a relationship low, or otherwise.

Emotions tend to take us to the edge, making us feel and act a little psycho, but when used right, those pesky feelings can work to your advantage.

All you have to do is meditate, curl your fingers, make a deep sound, and trust that what you're getting is better than a magic 8 ball.

It's easy, really. Feeling a little anxious about your boo? Anything can take us over the edge and no one knows it better than those of us in long distance relationships. Just the mention of another person of the opposite sex can send us into a confused frenzy where we make up all sorts of scenarios. Best thing to do is use your intuition in such cases. Calm your psycho ass down, take a deep breath, and put on some calming music for like five minutes. Close your eyes. See where it takes you. Trust the first thing that pops into your head, whatever it may be.

If you're still feeling a little off, listen to your thoughts. A lot of the time we get little hints and ideas about something we care about, and a lot of times those thoughts come from the psycho part of your brain, and others it comes from a deeper place.

Take recent events into consideration, especially if you've just insulted your boo's favorite football team because they suck, but now he's gone into Hulk mode and won't come down his testosterone-driven rant and is starting to take it to another level. He's having a fit. Because believe it or not, guys—even men—have fits. Just like when your nephew was three years old with a tendency to get what he wanted. Men have bitch-fits. And it's not your job to defuse it. It's not your job to backtrack whatever smart-ass emark you proudly said, especially if you don't want to. Don't. Don't do anything you don't want to do.

Instead, wait it out when you want to fight it out. Let him be a freaking baby about whatever he's being a baby about. Hang up the phone, laugh about the fact that your handsome, smart, funny man is also a freaking man-baby. Take that time to meditate, to remember the good times, to let yourself feel the love you (mostly) feel from him, and just ride the wave. When he calls you back and asks why you didn't call him back after hanging up, or why you didn't do anything but laugh, just say you let him have his bitch-it because that's what it was.

Instead of acting out your psycho, be intuitive. Let your intuition be your fire. That's how you can be scary without showing it, it's what gives you power over anyone without using your sexuality. It's how you rule, and no one knows how you do it.

Intuition gives you a leg up. It tells you everything you need to know, you just have to allow it. And once you do, your life will change so much.

- *Reminder*: Intuition is a bunch of things within you that work in unison to give you the answers you're looking for. It can range from what job to take (you know that feeling in the pit of your stomach you got when your now boss said you got the job? You should've listened to it, just look at you now), to what car to buy, to what food to eat, to what road to take. Have you ever had a moment of pure chance when you've taken a different way home, or avoided the highway you usually take for no reason? Then you come home, pour a glass of wine, eat your leftovers and watch the news to find there's been a huge accident on that highway? That moment, that little tiny moment that you decided to change your route, that was your intuition. You weren't blocking it with thoughts of *should I or shouldn't I*. You just let it happen and followed suit.

- *Hot Tip*: Having trouble letting go and just relax? Try taking a bubble bath with your favorite champagne. Play relaxing music, and just be. When you feel relaxed enough ask yourself questions you want answers to, and go with your first answer. Chances are what you want and what you're getting are contradicting each other and you're making excuses to get the answer you want. So, if the answer is to not get that job, don't. You may want the bigger paycheck, but the stress will not be worth it. Intuition works when you listen to it. It can help you avoid that job, and also avoid that fight.

- *Quick Tip*: Intuition is like a bicep. The more you use it, the stronger it gets.

Chapter 24

Keeping Your Options Open

....

There comes a time when trust and understanding wear out and all you want to do is drop him like a hot tamale. These feelings of another type of doubt may come at any time, mostly after a few months of the strain of a long distance relationship. You know a little more about your boo, you know things you probably didn't imagine about him on that dreamy first date, but here they are. He has a past, he has moods, he has feelings, he has flaws. He has it all. The good and the bad, and the ugly. He's human. But so are you.

So you find yourself on the hunt for a new adventure, a new book, a new boo to figure out. What's stopping you from looking? You're practically a single girl in a relatively big town, you're fucking hot (because you all are, trust!), you're funny, smart, driven, and any guy would be lucky to have your little pinky toe, let alone your cooch. You get checked out, and though that's nothing new, you find yourself liking it more and more. You get that little excited bubble in your chest and you want to dance and scream and date and kiss...

So, what's keeping you from keeping your options open? NOTHING. Girl, you may be loyal, you may be faithful, you may be freaking Sin The Saint, and even that can't stop you from looking if you want to. When the feeling hits, it hits. Girls will be girls, what are you going to do about it.

So, if you feel like looking, look. If you feel like straying, stray. If you feel like staying faithful, do. If you feel like doing whatever you want, by all means.

- *Reminder*: Remember to keep in mind that any action you take has a consequence, and cheating is never cool. If you find yourself noticing guys around you more than usual, take a moment to mull that over.
- Why are you all of a sudden noticing? What do you need/want that you're not getting? It's commonplace for our brains to focus on things that are familiar and things we *want*.
- So pay attention to what you find yourself paying attention to instead of just going by the motions. Ruminate, take your time, make a pro/con list, meditate, check in with your intuition, do yoga, take a bubble bath, take a walk in the park, take all the time you need, and when you figure it out, act on it.
- Be honest. Be real. Trust yourself. You know what you want, and you know what's best for you. So go and get it!

Chapter 25

Dum Dum Dum...
Cheating and its Ugly Snaky Head

....

Nobody likes liars.

Nobody.

No-one likes cheaters, and certainly no-one likes to be lied to and cheated.

So, if you're feeling the urge to cheat, here's a pro tip: don't. If you feel like cheating, take your happy ass home, open your laptop, FaceTime your boo, and tell him you're done. That's it. Don't send a text, don't write an email, don't Facebook message him, don't even call him, it deserves a face-to-face moment. And Skype, FaceTime, and even Snapchat can provide that for those of us with distance woes. So, don't try to get around it, delay it, or change it. Do it—cry, scream, yell, explain, cry some more, explain some more—but do it. Both of you will feel the needed closure.

Though it may suck, closure is needed. Then and only then can you start something new with someone new.

- *Hot Tip*: On the flip side, if your boo has ended things with you, there's only one thing to do: get revenge. *I'm serious*. And the best way to get revenge is to be better. Be happier. Be successful, be good. Live your life, get a hobby, go skydiving, take up golf, go snowboarding, take Kung Fu, boxing, read a lot, go to latin night and dance with strangers, go to Thunder from Down Under like your girlfriends have been suggesting, do it all.

- *Quick Tip*: The best revenge anyone can take is to improve themselves and be happy. Go snowboarding and tell no one, get an instructor and just go for it. Have you been afraid of open waters since Jaws? Take a snorkeling class or even better, take a scuba diving class. The worst that can happen is you meet people with different hobbies than you, and best that can happen is *you meet people with different hobbies than you*! So get out of your self-imposed shell and go do it!

- *Reminder*: Don't be a cheater. It never works for anyone, and the only thing that's achieved is a waste of time for you and your boo. Or ex boo. Because no matter what, truths have a way of coming to the light and when they do, it's not pretty. So be brave and break it off. It'll not only save you, it'll also save your soon-to-be-ex boo a lot of pain and suffering.

Chapter 26

Is He a Greek God or a Wilted Gyro?

....

So, cheating is not your style, but you're still feeling off and worn out. Maybe your Greek god is more of a wilted gyro, maybe you're just in a rut. Maybe when he called you today he said something that didn't rub you the right way. Maybe he mentioned a certain sexual act you're just not that interested in, and certainly don't want to try, maybe he even mentioned his ex had a way with it, and all that comment did was leave a sour taste in your mouth. Maybe it's not the first comment he's made that's less than classy. Maybe he's exhibiting the classic signs of A Bad Decision, and you're just starting to see it.

Take a moment to evaluate your feelings, because more often than not, they're trying to say something. And that something is always important. Listen to your gut (it's your intuition), because the more you listen to it, the more you can trust it, and the more it can guide you.

Trust yourself to keep going, and trust yourself to end it. You have power over your life, you make it happen. Everything is a choice and everything is *your* choice.

Unless he breaks up with you in which case, girl, you lucked out.

- *Hot Tip*: There's a quick and simple way to figure out a long and drawn out question or quandary you may find yourself in. If you find yourself not sure if you want to go on in the relationship, imagine yourself out of that relationship. Are you happy, are you free, are you finally able to breathe? There's your answer.
- On the flip side, are you sad, lonely, and depressed? Though that may not be your answer, it may be the beginning of a different issue you hadn't seen before.

- *Quick Tip*: Maybe he makes you happy 50% of the time, and the other 50% he makes you mad and angry or jealous. Imagine what the relationship would be like if he'd just stop talking about his past (or if he got the car he's been talking about nonstop, or called you more, texted more, or if he visited more, or whatever the problem may be). Are you happy, are you free, are you in love? If so, then there's your answer.

- *Reminder*: Though realizing you're happy 50% of the time may not mean your problems are solved, because you don't have control over your boo, you've come one step closer to figuring it out. When you do, talk about it. Maybe he finds that your attention to the relationship increases when he talks about his past, and he does it unconsciously. Maybe when he talks about his sexual past it gets a rise out of you and that makes him feel like you're more interested. If anything your partner is doing that bothers you, there's only one thing to do. Talk it out. Maybe then he'll understand that if he brings up his ex again you'll call it quits because there's no way you're competing with his past.

Chapter 27

In it to Win it:
So You've Decided to Keep Going, Now What?

....

You've had your doubts, you've overcome adversity, you've chosen love, so now what? You've made your decision. It was practically made for you, because who falls in love on purpose? If you really know what love takes, what it demands, what it expects, you wouldn't do it on purpose.

Especially when it's long distance.

Might as well sign up for experimental torture, really. Because long distance love is not the same as two-mile away love. It's not like your tenth-grade puppy love who lived a block away and the only one in the way was your mom because she made it impossible to escape the house after ten. It's not as cute, it's not as adorable, and certainly not as doable.

The kind of love you want takes time, hard work, dedication, and a certainty that can't be fabricated. It must come from that deeper part of the heart, that unguarded part of the brain, that unexplored, unexplainable part of emotions that can't be made into any sensible fact. Because it's unexplainable. It's unavoidable. It's crazy, and wild and real and honest and pure.

Love is always crazy anyway.

Who has ever made sense of love? Just ask history. No one. Not a one. Except maybe Kate Middleton and Prince William. That made sense, and I'm sure even they have problems. But you and your long distance boo probably won't make sense. They'll be a more sensible choice near you, in town, someone who knows your mom, maybe. And you'll be reminded of it all the time. I mean. All. The. Time. Either it will be your mother, your friends, your helpful ex, your newly engaged sister, your priest, your neighbor, or anyone who thinks they have it better than you because at least they're not pining for a love so far away. For a love so unattainable. For a love so inexplicable.

Strength, that's what you need. Strength. Conviction. Knowledge. Courage.

And most of all, love.

You need irrevocable love.

Chapter 28

Getting Hot and Heavy

....

You're in love. That's been established beyond doubt. Your mother may not be so happy, but if you hold her out with stories of your love adventures and where they have taken you, you might hold off until Thanksgiving, and that's what you're hoping for. You even threw in baking pies for people you hate to ease her troubles. Moving away might be worse, or so you tell her. Montana is miles, and miles away. Thanksgiving is just a stone throws distance. Your apartment is so much closer, you can practically walk to her place, pies in tow. She takes it, because that's all she can do. Helping her bake pies for Thanksgiving is her dream come true. And you oblige. You do the best damn job you are capable of, because you freaking care. You really do.

Your boo has been getting more open, and honestly it's a little hard to come to terms, because you had a certain idea of him, but the real thing is just so much more real. So much more honest. And maybe a little more than you planned to chew. But it's all good. He's getting a little hot, a little heavy. He's dropping the play, he's giving you the real deal. It's sort of easy, having him at arms length. But it's also a little hard having him so far away. So you develop ploys to keep you both sated—save a move states away.

And that's when you discover the naughty side of Skype, and Snapchat, and FaceTime. It's been there all along, you know this, but it hadn't been so freaking apparent before. You focused on your Skype meetings, your bare-faced snaps to your besties, and your nightly FaceTime with your boo. But up until this moment it hadn't been about seeing a real-time eggplant on your screen or how he whips it to and fro. It's all fun and games, you're enjoying your new extracurricular activities. A lot. Like, a whole lot.

And then he asks you for nudes.

Chapter 29

Should I Send Those
Naughty Pics He's Been Asking For?

....

It's all fun and games until he's the one asking you for naughty pics. There's a certain level of confidence that comes with sending cleavage pics, but another altogether when it comes to sending the tatas in their natural habitat, hanging free. Not that it's bad if it's your thing. By all means. Show those perky mountains off if you must. But for the rest of us, there's a line that's crossed when you're asked to reveal such a private part of yourself in such a disconnected way. Also, there's always the chance that you will break up and your risqué pics will end up on revenge pic sites or whatnot. There are plenty of movies with girls done wrong, let me tell you. So, yes. It is warranted if you feel guarded.

When it comes to exposing yourself (because that's what it feels like), you have to triple—no, quadruple—think it over. And then some more.

If he's patient he's a winner.

Your boo had to wait months for a naughty picture you felt comfortable sending. And you have to say, the riskier the pics, the less of your face and more of your hands in strategic places he saw. He thought it was sexy, like you were *feeling* yourself instead of hiding yourself. And you were, but you were also thinking about you and your clean reputation.

It wasn't him you didn't trust, it was society and technology. What if his best friend got into his phone in one of their infamous pranks against the other? What if he lost his phone and a hacker got into it? What if he left it unlocked at work and someone sneaked a peak at his photo album? What if he showed a decent picture of his dog to his coworker and he decided to swipe a few pics out and bam! There you are in all your naked glory. What if he set it as his home photo and your goodies were on display for any and all? It was these things that kept you decent. And it wasn't until you talked it out that you were comfortable enough to send anything you deemed risqué.

I mean, this is America after all, not France.

Though you're no prude, when it comes to you, you take your time and think it out. Feel it out. Ration it until it makes sense to you, and it stays true to you.

One thing that stands out in a long distance relationship is the lack of intimacy during your time apart. It's not news that people have been using multiple apps and websites to send naughty pics since the beginning of the internet. It's a way to feel closer, to share, to please, to be pleased. It's great and it's dangerous and it's exciting, I know this. You know this. We all know this. But there are lines you don't want to cross and there are lines you shouldn't cross. If you feel uncomfortable sending permanent pictures of your tatas, but feel comfortable sending a three-second Snapchat, do so. If you feel comfortable sending the permanent photo, send it. If you don't, don't.

Don't you get talked into it, either. Haven't we all heard about professional women, famous women, even celebrities in undesirable positions after a leaked nude photo showed up? Haven't we had enough warning stories to keep us thinking smart? Like that one teacher who got suspended for just having nude selfies on her phone her students happened to come across. It's a slippery slope.

- ◆ *Reminder:* It's all about trust. If you trust your boo, if you want to send those pics, if it makes you happy, do it! You and you alone are the ruler of your existence! If you're doubtful, scared, pressured, bullied, talked into, if you're feeling even a modicum of doubt, wait it out. Don't ever do something you don't want to just to prove your love. If he loves you, he will wait, he will do without, he will trust you, and even so still love you. Think about it. Talk it out. You're with your boo because you love him, trust him, and you've learned communication is key. So talk about your feelings, your doubts, your fears, and lay it all out. You'll know what to do. You'll feel it in your gut (intuition).

Chapter 30

Being a Bad Girlfriend and Sending Pussycat Pics

....

What constitutes being a good girlfriend and the opposite, a bad girlfriend? Is it refusing to send pussycat pics that makes you a bad (long distance) girlfriend? Is it sending them that makes you a good girlfriend?

It all comes down to how you want to see the situation. If you're the kind of person who feels super confident in sending pictures of your precious over some metal wires (is that how it works?) to your boo, then good on you.

If you're a little more guarded, then listen up, biatches, because I'm about to let you know how it's done.

So your boo won't shut the fuck up about your precious and the stupid ass picture he wants and you're like, are you fucking kidding me, asshole? I had enough trouble sending you those naughty pics of my more-than-usual-exposed cleavage, now you want a pussy pic?

Because that's how it works.

One minute it's "I promise I won't ask for more," and the next "Please send it, pretty pretty please with sugar on top," because the asshole is going to want more. You give a hand and they take the whole damn arm. You give in to one and then bam! Everything else is up for grabs.

Fear not, pussycat guarders, because there are ways to get around that stupid ass request. All you have to do is be wittier, smarter, and smoother than your boo.

Here's what you do when your boo asks that stupid ass request: Google kitty underwear pictures, find a girl wearing one (with her skirt up, all cutesy tootsey, trust me —you'll find it) and send it. I mean, he wants pussy, he gets pussy, right? It won't be you, and it won't be what he wanted, but at least he'll get it, won't he?

Okay, so here's the deal. If your boo wants to see a pussycat, all he has to do is log into the naughtier part of the internet and he'll have plenty for days. There is no reason to want to see yours. They don't all look the same, but damn, doesn't he have an imagination or long term memory? Bottom line is, if you felt uncomfortable sending tatas through picture, you sure as hell aren't going to feel comfortable with exposing your most precious and delicate place, are you? Nooooo.

Now, you're all up for a good time, don't get me wrong. It's so fun, sending naughty pics, sexy pics, you even bought lingerie to do photo shoots. But what you don't feel comfortable with, what you don't deem sexy, what you don't want to do, you don't.

Hey, at least he got a pussycat pic. He did. He can't say he didn't.

◆ *Reminder:* We all know this very simple rule: Fuckboys ask for pussy pics, long distance boyfriends know better. So if your long distance boyfriend is feeling a little fuckboyish, then let him know how you feel and he better get it or you're going to be hunting for your next boyfriend come next weekend. Or swiping right for your next boytoy, whatever.

Chapter 31

Do You Really Like His Dick Pics?

....

If there's one thing to say about nudes is that guys feel a whole lot more comfortable sending them than girls do. Or at least than you do, right? But do you really enjoy getting that phallus picture all erect and at attention?

You have to be honest here and admit that—yes, yes you do! It's not a freaking crime to enjoy your partner in the nude—if, and only if he feels comfortable sending such delicate and personal pictures. It all goes down to (ahem, no pun intended) really enjoying him—all of him.

Which is one of the reasons you sent some of your more risqué pictures to begin with, if you did at all. If you're enjoying his ugly dick pics, then you can see how he would enjoy your more fleshy ones, too. It is not an every day thing. He doesn't flood your phone with his little (no, it's big, I swear) statue.

It's all about feelings, about mood, about connection. Sometimes you can be on FaceTime watching a movie on Netflix for hours and nothing risqué happens, and it's perfect and pretty and lovely and all, and sometimes you can't even get a decent hello before you're going at it. It's all a nice balance of hormones, mood, and emotions.

- ◆ *Hot Tip*: On the flip side, what if you're not enjoying his little statue? What if he floods you with unwanted peckers all day every day? Tell him! If you've gotten this far, it should be so freaking obvious by now that yes, communication is key! So speak up, say your mind, and watch him acquiesce to your liking.

Can You Really Live Without Them?

....

The dong pics, I mean. And the truthful answer is yes, you can. You can live without his pecker in you face when you FaceTime, without his little (big) statue greeting you after dinner, without his mini-boo erect and at attention at midnight when you can't sleep, without his one-eyed snake shaking it off when you're feeling particularly naughty—but do you want to? No. Not really.

You enjoy his manhood. You enjoy watching him do the things he does even when you're not there. You imagine you love it as much as you would love giving him a little mouth action in the morning as a way of waking him up, or after you push him on the couch to have your way with him and unzip his jeans, the ones you love on him, and his little (big) statue meets you, hard and ready. You imagine it's like that.

You enjoy his dick pics. You thoroughly enjoy them. They're the next-best-thing you have, and you fucking enjoy them. You're that weirdo girlfriend who actually asks for them when it's gone a week without a new angle, a new view. Yes you can live without them, but why would you? You like receiving them.

You love them, in fact.

Chapter 32

Snapchatting and Long Distance Relationships

....

There hasn't been a more deserving godsend for couples with distance woes as Snapchat (of Snap Inc. Is it now?) has been a gift from above. Sure, there's text, pictures, FaceTime, and whatnot. But there's something more alluring about the fact that you're never going to see what you just saw ever again. I mean, EVER AGAIN. How enticing is that? So fucking enticing. You'll see what he sends a million times in person throughout your life, but at that moment, in that context, never again. It'll last ten seconds. That's it. I mean, what if someone told you you can eat cheesecake for ten seconds and ten seconds only? It would be a ten second heaven. One that can't be had ever again in the same manner. It's a once in a lifetime thing. And it's appreciated immensely.

The rush that accompanies sending a Snap is also as alluring—even more so—than receiving. It's something your boo will see only once, have to commit it to memory if he wants to recall it, or take a screenshot (and the alert that he has done so is another type of feeling altogether), and that makes you so freaking hot you can't explain it. It's a relationship thing. You send Snaps all day—silly faces, songs you're listening to, cute filtered selfies, unashamed makeup free, bun wearing, grocery shopping selfies to your besties—but when you send you boo a special snap, you've done it. Because you know how much he'll appreciate it.

- ◆ *Hot Tip*: Send him a cute snap without him expecting one. Maybe he's getting his hair cut at the barber, and after that he'll be going to his friend's house to pick up his toolbox and you know he'll be distracted—send him a cute selfie! It'll remind him you're thinking of him, and cut through the boring everyday things he has to do. Plus, he'll appreciate the cute gesture.

- ◆ *Quick Tip*: Feeling frisky when your boo is at work? Have a photoshoot and send him more risqué Snapchats (just make sure he's alone when he opens them!), he'll not only love them, but appreciate you more for them.

To Use or Not to Use Filters

....

There has recently been a backlash against using filters in pictures on Instagram, Snapchat, pretty much anywhere you can post pictures to, and all I have to say to that is —screw that! Filters are there for us to use them, so why the hell not?

So the right Snapchat filter gives you clearer skin, so what. It's still you, just with baby-smooth skin. Like an airbrushed version of your less than perfect skin. They even have some with doggie ears and it's adorable and you send your boo that one all the time. They also have one with little butterflies that thins out your face and makes you look like the goddess you are, so yes. Excuse you the fuck out, but yes, use them. And love them.

You can even use them on days when you're feeling low about your face, maybe you had a breakout during that time of the month, and you don't want to take a picture, but when you see that smoothed out look, you feel brave enough to send it. So yes, use them, and love them, and no-one can tell you not to.

- *Hot Tip*: Feeling a little down? Tap that favorite filter of yours, the one that makes you look doe eyed with clear skin and higher cheekbones. Take a selfie you freaking love, one you save to your memories section, and send it to your boo. He'll love it. And he won't bitch at you for using a freaking filter.

Chapter 33

Is it Okay to Have Phone Sex?

....

The real question is: is it okay NOT to have phone sex? Because let me tell you, if you're months out into a long distance relationship, you're way overdue. So go ahead. Give in. Make some noises, touch yourself a little, play a little, make him feel wanted, make her feel adored, tell him how much you miss him, tell her how much you love her voice, and just do it. You know you want to.

If you have been having phone sex all along, know this: You're not alone. Most couples in a long distance relationship need to have this connection to feel closer, more connected, more in tune. So if you've been holding back, let go. Let go, and live a little. What's the harm? The only thing that can stem from this is you becoming closer and your boo becoming addicted to you and how you make him feel.

- *Hot Tip*: When in the depths of passion, try closing your eyes and shutting off that part of your brain that analyzes everything, and just let go. Give in. Give it everything you have, because then and only then is it a real, connecting passion.

- *Reminder*: If you have roommates or thin walls, make sure you're only loud enough for your boo to hear your crazy, out of this world moaning through the phone, not your apartment complex. We all know it's you making you sound like that, so take it down a notch. But really, it's also his voice and his sounds that make you go crazy, so let go, but be mindful. You know when it's too loud and when it's just right. Find that happy balance.

Chapter 34

How to Dirty Talk When it Feels Awkward as Fuck

....

Phone sex can mean more than just moaning and the occasional grunt and dirty word to get things going. The whole experience has been a little challenging for you, it's okay to admit it.

Not that you're a prude (you're not!), but your boo has occasionally asked you to say dirty things in the heat of the moment, and more often than not, you blanked. I mean, what does talking dirty mean, anyway! What does it mean? It can mean many things to different people, so again, I cannot stress enough how important communication is between the two of you. Find what works, toss what doesn't, and take it from there.

There comes a time when you say things you never thought you would say, things that work for him, but make you giggle. Breathe through those moments of doubt, of disconnect. If you're not feeling it, your boo will know. They have this sixth sense about these kinds of things. Like that time you were pretending and he figured you out in .2 seconds. They know and they will always know. Vice versa, you'll also know if he's less than interested in saying some of the things that turn you on. So talk it out. Ask him what he likes to hear.

Guys can be more crude than women, so if he asks for something extra nasty, it may just be that it's what works for him. If you don't feel particularly comfortable, try saying something along the lines you do feel comfortable with instead.

Try saying things that turn *you* on. The cadence and tone you use will work for all intents and purposes. Saying something you don't feel okay with can often times lead to a moment-killer, so trust yourself, trust your gut, and trust your emotions. He will understand if saying you want him to come all over your face is not something that makes you as hot as it does him. And if he doesn't, remind him you're classy unlike his stupid exes.

- *Reminder*: Let go of your insecurities. Chances are they're just in your head and he can't see them or rationalize them. So let go, give into the moment. Stop thinking, let go and just *be.* And if something is still causing you trouble, try something else.

- *Example*: "Tell me you want me to come all over your face, baby," he says, but you're not feeling it. "How about I come all over your face?" you say. "Oh, damn, you're going to squirt all over me? Hell yeah." And he's happy, and you're happy. The end.

Chapter 35

How to Take Charge of Your Sexuality

....

We are sexual beings. From the crown of our head to the tip of out toes, we are sexual. Sex can be casual, it can be fun, it can be sexy, it can be sensual, it can be passionate, it can take over your mind, body and being, and take you to dimensions you had no idea about. It can also keep you closely guarded, almost like in a prisoner of your own mind, your own insecurities, your doubts. It can be the greatest, and at times it can be the hardest to let go and enjoy.

Everyone has sensuality in them, everyone has sexuality within them, and everyone is passionate. What better way to show that side of you than with your chosen partner?

It can be extremely hard for long distance partners to find an elevated sensuality in sexual activities because of obvious reasons, but even through the distance, the hardships, the phone line or the video chat, sensuality and passion can be achieved, and they must. They absolutely must. Not just to feel closer through the distance, but to be closer in spirit, in mind, and in soul.

- *Hot Tip*: Take charge of your thoughts. If your mind is on the awkwardness of the moment, the camera on your face, the fact that you're alone, the groceries you have to get, the project you have to finish, the meeting at work, the calls you have to make—you're never going to let go and become that sensual person you want to be. So take charge, let go of everything around you, forget about the phone on your hand or the laptop beside you. Focus instead on the handsome man on the screen—better yet, imagine there is no screen. Imagine it's just you and your boo. Imagine and feel it in your core.

- *Quick Tip*: A huge tip when it comes to the bedroom with any couple—in person or far away—is to synch your breathing. That can be easier done in person, feeling his rising chest and his exhale matching yours, but totally doable over the phone or Skype or FaceTime. Don't be afraid of telling your boo to hear your breathing, listen to it, match it. And at the same time, listen to his, feel his heart through his breath, become one. And watch your world disappear and your souls collide.

- *Reminder*: A sexual human being is a healthy human being.

Let go and Live a Little

....

If you still find yourself having trouble with your sensuality, consider this: What are you afraid of? That you may be vulnerable to a partner of your choice? You already are. In every level you are. Are you afraid of yourself? If it's not with your current boo, miles apart, it will be with someone else close together. Don't let fear dictate what you do. If you really want this, you can have it. It's just about making up your mind about it, letting go, and not be afraid of a little vulnerability.

Also, what kind of stories do you want to tell your grandchildren? That you chickened out on a little solo moment of passion with your boo on the line? Or that you gave it your all and now here they are? I'd choose the latter. On Thanksgiving. While slicing pie I baked myself.

♦ *Hot Tip*: Get out of your head. That is the worst and best advice anyone could ever give. How do you get out of your head? In person, it would be by turning out the lights and letting your body guide you. On the phone, however, it's a whole different ballpark. The best thing you can do is GET OUT OF YOUR HEAD. You're the only one judging yourself. You're the only one wondering if you said the right thing or if he's into it. If he's a flesh and blood man who has the hots for you, pretty much whatever you say is going to work. So give it a try! Close your eyes and let the moment guide you, not your thoughts. Close your eyes and use that overactive imagination to your advantage, because you want to. You know you do.

Chapter 36

Nicknaming His Johnson

....

There comes a time in every couple's relationship where it becomes something more concrete, more honest, more special. It's an invisible line that's crossed, a milestone, a turn of a leaf, a new chapter. But it's there, and it brings you closer. That moment is when you name his Johnson—his manhood, his little statue, his woodpecker, his jackhammer...whatever you want to call it.

Nothing brings you closer than convincing him his little statue is now called Tyrone. Nothing. He will fight you on this. Do not relent. He will try to convince you to name it Big Aaron, Huge Johnson, Aaronhead (actually, I liked that one), Batman Foreskin, Suicide Squirt, Jokerjack, and others, but if you want Tyrone, it will be Tyrone.

And it will make you closer because he will know the power you have. And that power is beautiful.

Accepting Nicknames for Your Pussycat

....

Yes, you have a power that cannot be replicated and cannot be refuted.

But so does he.

Sorry. It's true.

So after you call his mini "Tyrone" he will retaliate, and he will get what he wants.

He will call your cooch whatever he wants, but you have to agree. It's a battle of who's the more stubborn of the two. He'll start with Ava-kitkat, and you will say no. Then he'll move on to Harley Quim, Mermaid purse, Cookie, Cara Mia, Treasure Island, and others, then he will go back to Ava-kitkat and you'll say yes because it's better than fucking Harley Quim.

And he will show you he also has a veritable force that cannot be refuted.

Chapter 37

Communication Woes

....

There comes a time in every couple's experience when you've outdone it. Maybe you've talked on the phone every day for three weeks straight. Maybe you've Skyped every night without miss. Or maybe you've recounted your childhood favorite movies for the fifth time this week, and the conversation is getting a little stale. You've stopped sleeping your regular hours, work is suffering as a result, and when he calls that little stir you felt in your belly is now turning to an unexpected groan.

You need your time to recoup, relax, make more stories to tell. Maybe you just need a good night out with your girls, or a freaking brunch with your mom without a distracting call. Whatever it may be, you're worn out. You need a breather, and you need it bad.

If you're feeling worn out and stretched thin, worry not! Chances are your boo is feeling the same. Unless he's a loner with no family, your boo is probably dying for some alone time, or quality time with his friends and family. Time when it's just him with his crazy friends making memories, or time with his baby nephew, building stories to tell you later—much, much later.

And you—well, you're planning on getting your nails done with your ratchet (but fun as hell) girls. You need a change, a different story to tell, that telltale feeling in your gut that you're about to make memories to last you a few good years. That kind of debauchery that only comes about every so often, and you've been depriving yourself because you've been sitting at home talking to your boo who's miles, and miles away (his choice, btw) while your girls live it up. Enough is enough. You're about to explode with pent up energy, and it's your time to let it out.

- *Hot Tip*: If it's your boo telling you he needs a day, a night, a weekend to himself, realize he's not cutting you off. Dig deep within yourself, and realize you're pining for that time too. You need it. Take it. Go crazy, drink tequila, wear a skirt the night you go to that bar with the mechanical bull. Live it up. Why not?

- *Reminder*: On the flip side, if it's you who needs a breather, this is the time to be brutally honest. Not brutal, just brutally honest. So many times, being honest can be brutal in itself—especially if it's directed towards a loved one. Get your big girl panties on, breathe, and do. Tell your boo how you feel. Your conversations are getting recycled.
- It's probable he'll agree, too.
- You want to go out, but no, you don't want to get your face slapped by twenty Mandingo dicks. You just don't. Not that you're judging, but that's not your end goal. All you want is a nice night out with your girls, a few drinks, a little booty

shakin' near total strangers, a little bull riding (the mechanical kind, duh). You need to live it up a little, all you need is a few days. That's all. Just a few days and then it's back to the grind with your boo. Chances are you'll miss him so much, you'll call him out of the blue, get freaky, say stuff you've never said before —and isn't that the best?

Chapter 38

How Many Texts are Too Many?

....

So you're in a long distance relationship, and the constant communication thing is starting to weigh heavy around your pretty little neck. Now what? Should you tell him all those Skype calls are taking it's toll? He's obviously not a texter, you know. How about you just text him instead, just today, you swear. Just so you can get some stuff done around the house before his nightly call that always turns into phone sex. But you've already texted him ten times before he responded because he was at a meeting and you still want to communicate but a phone call is too much of a commitment at the moment. You've already texted, and you want to text some more. So just how many texts are too many?

None. That's it. Let's move on to the next topic because this one is pretty much done. I'm being quite serious. Texting is the easiest, most convenient form of communication, and doing it over and over again is perfectly perfect.

Some people say too much communication will exhaust a long distance relationship. It's true with many forms of communication all wrapped up into one big bundle of overdone joy.

Texting throughout the day, doable. Nightly phone calls are doable. Skype calls every two days are doable. FaceTiming when you're shopping and take a break at the coffee shop, doable. Snapchat after Snapchat is doable, but put all of those together and you've got yourself a full-time job. Too much of a good thing gets boring, and overdone.

Phone calls can be exhausting. They entail actually cutting time out of your day, busy or no, to talk. Sometimes it's doable, others not so much. Especially when you have a particularly tight deadline or get in those crazy, gotta-clean-my-house-now moods. Skype can be even worse, let's not get started. I mean, that means your makeup has to be on point (or that beard has to be at least roughly combed for the guys, or makeup if that's your thing), your bedroom or living room or kitchen or wherever your choose to Skype from has to be spotless, and your cleavage has to be high and proud (again, beard for the guys reading). It's a freaking chore!

Text, however, is so much more chill. Like so, so chill. You can be in the freaking bathroom, peeing, or taking a bath, or reheating your leftover takeout, or shaving your legs (or growing out that beard, guys), or trying the latest face mask out and your boo wouldn't be the wiser. You can be doing whatever you please and the text will still get to you, and you will respond. That's how it goes.

So, unless you're sending a hundred unanswered text back-to-back, you're good. Keep going. It's more than likely your boo also understands the quick and easy form of communication texts allows, and more than likely he also needs some time to get things done around his house, too.

◆   *Reminder:* That is not to say that endless phone calls and the occasional FaceTime isn't a good thing. Who doesn't love seeing their boo even through the small screen? If it's a phone call, go for it. Who can't plug in some headphones (or use those wireless ones) and get things done while still talking to your boo. If it's going to be a Skype call, give plenty of heads up, because looking camera ready is not easy—even for the small screen.

Chapter 39

What if He Doesn't Text as Much as You'd Like?

....

Unfortunate are those who "hate texting" (like my freaking boo). Unfortunate indeed. Because no matter how much your boo hates texting, he will always get a text. I kid you not, this girl can text in her sleep—like most people living in the 21st century. So, if you're stuck with a non-texter like me, try a few simple fool-proof ways to get him to text more.

- ◆   *Hot Tip*: Texting can be hard—no, no it can't! It's the easiest thing anyone can do.
- ◆   Sending that first text, however, can be tricky stuff if not done right. So, what's the best way to start a text convo with your boo? Here are some fool-proof ways to get you started:

   1. Instead of starting with the usual (overdone and boring) "hey," try to change it up a bit, especially if you want the conversation to keep going. Send him a video of something funny or a music video to get the conversation started. If he's as cool as you think he is, he'll go along with it perfectly. On the other hand, if he's a dud, try something else to get his texting prowess to show. Does he love sports? Send him a link to the latest gossip on his favorite team and give it your own little thought. You know him best, so give it a try and see how it goes.

   2. If you know your boo has a particularly busy day, like on the days your boo has to work 12-hour shifts, send him some cute shit. He'll eat that up like no other. Something along the lines of... "Good morning, baby. I hope you have an amazing day thinking of me and that little spaghetti top you love so much..." Or, "I'm counting the hours until I get to talk to you! I'll be thinking of you doing that thing you do..." Or, "I really appreciate all you do for us, baby. I love love love you!" You know what you like, sound like, and whatnot. Don't be afraid to let it out. You're in a freaking long distance relationship after all, okay. So just go. Go do it. Now.

   3. At times you'll be out living life and your boo will be all that ways away living life or trying to. The best way to make someone feel loved and desired is to include him in your life, whatever that may be. Have family visiting from California? Text him and text him again and again until you break your texting record. How do you do it? I mean, you have family over. You're hosting so that means you have your parents (whom you love), your sisters (love), aunts (love/like), cousins (love/like), and even some

distant cousins (ummm, yeah, you can do without) over. It's an art, really. Every time a distant cousin does or says something funny or weird or just outright creepy, text your boo. It'll be like an inside joke that just keeps going. You'll say, "Oh, jeez. Now he's trying to get me to open a medical marijuana store. Save me!" He'll say something like, "Hahahaha I can just see you as a drug dealer. Feisty and mean. Damn, sexy as hell." Or whatever. Make it fun, make it alluring, make it easy and soon enough you'll have your boo eating off your hand. Or just texting you a lot more, you know.

4.   A true and tested favorite: Send him a picture of yourself. This is where it can go any which way you want, really. If you want to be cute, send him a cute Snap with that little dog filter that makes your skin unbelievably smooth, the one you love so much, you basic skank (just kidding. That's only the media that makes you out to look like that. If you want to use the fucking doggie filter, by god you'll freaking use it). If you want to get naughty, send him a pic of you biting your lip or licking your finger, whatever floats your boat. If you want to get down and dirty, send him a little peek of the panties you're waring. Get it, girl! He'll love it so much, he'll have no other choice but to text you back.

5.   Whatever you decide to send, be it a text, a picture, a video, a link to an article you just read, a funny thing that's happening around you, be yourself! Let your star shine bright, even if it's through text. It's so informal that it can be manipulated to work for your every whim. Give it a try.

Chapter 40

What if He's More of a Calling Person?

....

Texting is cool, guys. I mean, it's so freaking cool, EVERYONE does it. Some people, however, are still more fond of calling. It's not that he's secretly a ninety-year old man disguised as a young, crazy hot man you met a year ago on the Strip drinking an Eiffel Tower slushy and have been in a long distance relationship with ever since.

It just means your boo likes to hear your voice. Plain and simple.

You've texted. A lot. You've turned him around with the whole text thing, but calling is still his go-to mode of communication. You've tried to change it, maybe just a little bit, but it hasn't really taken. He's texting, he's responding to your texts, but it's few and far in between the hour-long phone calls at lunch time. At least he makes you laugh. And he is texting more, if not as much as you'd prefer, he's doing it. Especially on those long days when talking has to wait. Texting is doing it's job keeping you connected, keeping you in the know.

It's just like your brother in California. You text, he calls you to respond. It takes precious minutes from your life, but you love it. Because you love him and you love the communication and effort he puts into it.   Just like your brother, your boo still calls you. You still answer. You swoon—again—at the sound of his voice. Then he tells you something funny and you laugh. He laughs.

That's it. Right there. He tells you he loves it, you ask what, he says your laugh. You have the best laugh, he says, and you blush even though he can't see it. You blush even after all these months. And you say you love his laugh, too, and his voice...oh, his voice. And he says he needs to hear it every day, all day if he could. And you agree. And then right there, in that moment, you get it.

Calling is calling and texting is texting. He's been right all along, but you're never going to admit it. You'll just enjoy the benefit of knowing he loves your laugh. So go ahead and do it more. Laugh until the sun rises again. Laugh until it hurts. Laugh and love and live, because even though you're so far away in miles, you're just a phone call away from hearing his voice.

Chapter 41

What if He Complains
About the Number of Texts You Send or Calls You Make?

....

You're making an effort, you know you are. You text, you call. You Skype, you Snapchat. You leave voice messages, and video ones too. You love talking to your boo, you just do. You do it over and over again because feeling close to him is more than just thinking about him, it's getting his responses, hearing his voice, seeing his handsome face, hearing his laugh, getting his silly Snapchats.

It's all good and well, but what if he complains it's all just too much? What if he complains you send too many texts he can't even think, too many calls he doesn't have time for, too many video messages you're leaving for him that he doesn't have time for, too many selfies left unseen?

Sometimes you gotta dig deep. So deep it hurts. So deep you have the answer staring at you in the face, smacking you over and over, yet still refuse to see the answer. What's the most important thing in a long distance relationship? I'll give you a chance to come up with your own answer. Go. Get it.

Got it? Here it is: Communication. Communication, communication and then some. There will be times in our life we want something that's so unattainable, we hold on to it because we're stubborn, because we're masochists, because we love hurting ourselves. We try to make it something it's not—more than what it is. In the end we only end up hurting ourselves.

If your boo is not on the same page as you, talk about it. Ask your boo what he or she truly wants. Are they in it to win it or just for fun? Is it just a pastime to them, just to hold them out until the real thing comes along? Because your time is so much more valuable than just for fun.

You're in it, you devote time, effort, love, feelings, emotions, and so much more that if your boo is not giving the same, trying the same or appreciating what you do, take time to evaluate things and reevaluate them again. Make a decision and keep it. Don't be played a fool, and don't play either. No one has time for that kind of shit.

♦   *Hot Tip*: If your boo complains about the amount of communication you're requesting, drop his ass! There's nothing in the world worse than you wanting more than he's willing to give or wanting to get. You have so much to give, and if he's not happy about being on the receiving end, someone else will. You are beautiful inside and out, with so much to give, and a truly deserving man will see that and hold on to it like a tongue on a freezing pole. Trust.

Chapter 42

Different Forms of Communication
to Keep in Touch When Your Boo is Miles Away

....

Nowadays, it is so easy to reach out and talk to someone. I can talk to my friend in Germany through Skype, WhatsApp, Snapchat, email, and not even pay a cent more for the services. That's all thanks to people like Alexander Graham Bell of the telephone, Vinton Cerf and Robert Kahn of the World Wide Web, Steve Jobs and Tim Cook of Apple, Bill Gates of Microsoft, Mark Zuckerberg of Facebook, Evan Spiegel of Snapchat (Snap Inc.), Brian Acton and Jan Koum of WhatsApp, Niklas Zennström of Skype, Kevin Systrom of Instagram, and Tom Anderson of Myspace (remember that?). Thanks to them and many, many others, we have this great gift of easy peasy communication and connection. So when in a long distance relationship, don't be afraid to try them all and find what fits best.

Maybe you'll find that the best form for you is Snapchat and it's ten second videos that your boo will never see again. Maybe it's Line text where you send endless emojis. Maybe it's setting up your PlayStation and talking through your headset, even though he kills way more zombies than you, but he revives you all the time and you love him for it. Maybe it's good old fashioned phone calls when watching a movie he gave you the code to download on your iTunes and you play at the same time, you even count down to press play. There are so many ways of communication, and not one of them is bad. Well, except email. For the love of love, don't email.

You know how I'm always saying communication is key? Well there you go. Communicate. Talk. Show. Include. Text. Play. Snap. Instagram. Facebook. Whatever you want, just do it.

Chapter 43

A Question on Facebook, an Answer on Instagram

....

The one drawback to so many forms of communications is the back and forth between them all. You can ask a question on Facebook about the dates he has off next month, and get an answer on your Instagram selfie. Then he'll Snapchat you a cute selfie with his dog next to him asking what you're having for dinner tonight, and your phone reminds you you're at 10% so you charge your phone and forget to respond, then remember to answer when you're on texting your girls so you send a quick text.

It's exhausting. It's like a group text you want to kill. It's like the Instagram DM you forget to answer to, then feel bad about two weeks later, like the Snap you forgot to respond to, the What'sApp you ignored. It can be too much.

- *Quick Tip*: If you find yourself in one of these Social Media webs of death, figure out what's best for the two of you and do those. If you find that you like sending a cute Snapchat more because the pictures adds a little more than just texting, make Snapchat your go-to method of quick communication. If you feel like the virtual closeness of Skype or video messages work best, do that instead. Decide what works for both of you to avoid jumping around from app to app.

Chapter 44

Accepting The Good, The Bad, and The Ugly

....

We all have layers. Like Shrek said, we're like onions. Layer after layer of facets and emotions, of likes and dislikes, of wants and fears, goals and dreams, love and hate, passion and action, creation and destruction. We have it all. But do we go to our favorite coffee shop wearing all of our onion layers for all? Noooo. No fucking way. It's human nature to hide the deepest and scariest part of ourselves. To hide them so deep, we can't even recognize them as our real selves. Hide them so well, that it takes us by surprise when we show even a sliver of who we really are.

So if we don't know ourselves as we think we do, how do we expect to know who our partner is without getting the good along with the bad? The goods are good. Great sex, good talks, undeniable chemistry—that's all the good we love and want more of. So much more of. But what about the moods, the fears, the reactions, the peeling of the good layers, the ones we like to show—what about those?

It came as a huge surprise to find your boo was not perfect. It was an even bigger surprise to find *you* weren't perfect. You had him in person for two months. Sure, that's not a long time by any stretch, but you knew him. You had an idea of who he was. You liked who he was—who he showed you he was in those two months. He also got an idea of you and what you wanted to show him.

There's a veil that can't be seen when getting to know someone. It's a veil that keeps all those deeper layers hidden, away from everyone who isn't privy to them. That veil is called politeness. Unless you're dating the Son of Satan, there's bound to be a veil. Trust. It's there.

Something magical, however, happens when you date a man who lives a thousand miles away. That magic is what clears that veil, and all those real tidbits of onion layers start to peel off and show.

It's like when your boo calls you out for being selfish. It's the first you're hearing of this (at least to your face), even though cousin Hannah probably would agree because of that one time you didn't want to share your Hot Cheetos with her in the second grade. And rightfully so. That skank had two more dollars than you did, and didn't want to spend them. Now she's living the life of your dreams if only for two weeks a year because she's so freaking cheap and saves all year long for her vaca, but who's watching anyway. Stupid Instagram pictures of stupid Bora Bora and blah blah blah.

Anyway, he's called you selfish and you gasp because no man has ever had the *cojones* to call you that (again to your face) and survive. But he has the advantage of living a thousand miles away. So you listen instead of stab him with a fork. You ask how he could possibly think you're selfish, you're nothing but giving and kind and *giving*! And he says yes, you are, but you give in a calculated manner that makes you selfish because you're eyeing your end result. And that right there you'd never know if it wasn't for that a-hole who found it useful to call you out. And then he tells you that you like picking fights when you're bored and all of a sudden you see all your past relationships flash before your eyes and it hits you like a ton of freaking lipsticks because you just realize you're a saboteur.

You've deliberately, but unconsciously, sabotaged every single relationship you've ever had. Every. Single. One. And thanks to that a-hole who has you all figured out, now you know.

Just as he's seen, heard, observed, and figured out your dirty little secrets, you also have your treasure chest of misdeeds your boo probably has no idea he is the proud owner of. It starts with the uncommonly bad mood he's in after work. Especially when he has to work a 12-hour shift and he calls you on the way home from work—it's like talking to the freaking Demon of Anger, if there is such a one. He's short-worded and pissy, and he takes on average twelve minutes to cool off.

He hates his job, and he doesn't even know it. You hold on to this information until you can't take it anymore. It's either he quits his job and finds one he loves, or he stops calling you after those long shifts because it's not cool and it's not okay.

So you tell him he hates his job and he goes on a rant about how much he cares for his job and appreciates it. It pays the bills, doesn't it? So you tell him that so would another job.

Slowly he realizes, without wanting to, that indeed he does hate his job. The next time he calls you after a long shift he's aware of his sour mood and suddenly it clicks and he finally resolves to find a better, more rewarding job. Then you tell him he likes to watch Deadpool a hundred times because in his mind he is Ryan Reynolds and wants his life. He doesn't argue.

That's how you two have become each other's psychologists, therapists, and counselors.

You love the good, accept the bad, and find the ugly. When you still love everything about your boo, when even after seeing all the layers he has to offer you still love him. That right there is true love.

Chapter 45

Fights Happen to Us All

....

You're not safe from a good fight whether you're perfect for each other or not. You know what I'm talking about, the kind of fight where you mess up your vocal chords ending forever the illusion you could ever sing like Beyoncé, the kind where you find that yes you could've played softball if you wanted to with that arm of yours, and that you're pretty good at insults, that kind of fight. And when it's over the phone, it's just the same. Trust me.

I know what you're going to say. Can't you just hang up the phone, cut the Skype call, or just don't send that Snap, but no. That's not enough. Fights are when the real meaty substance of the relationship truly shows.

You call him out for abandoning you because you never asked for a long distance relationship. You were duped. He calls you out for your attitude. At first he called your "attitude" cute, strong, sassy, *fun*. Now it's you're a bratty adult with a devil attitude, but whatever. So, no. You don't hang up. You stay and you fight because he said he likes American bacon and you say you like veggie bacon and you're going to win, damn it. But now it has turned into a fight to the death because he called you bratty and you called him out for abandoning you. And so it begins.

Fights can start from anywhere. About anything. At any given time. And it will always go back to what's really on your respective minds. He thinks your attitude could be different, that you're a little rude, a little spoiled. You think he should've never left, you resent him for it, and it shows every time you fight.

That's how fights can be good. They can be eye opening. All you have to do is listen. I mean, of course you're going to put your two cents in, but you're also listening. Learning.

No way you're going to fix your attitude, because that's what makes you you. So you talk it out. No he doesn't want you to change. He just wants you to be a little nicer, a little more understanding. So you talk some more. He can't move back to Las Vegas, can't move back to you. At least not yet, he says. He's so close to finishing what he started. He's so close to getting his son. You take a deep breath and relax because you know it's the right thing to do. It'll never be over. He'll always have to be there for his son, he'll always have to fight with is ex, it'll be a never ending story. But you want him, you love him, and you respect him.

◆ *Hot Tip*: Fights happen to us all. There is no one relationship that has ever survived without a good, balls to the ceiling fight. So take it in stride. If you find that you two are constantly fighting, recognize the main problems that arise and try to work them out. It won't be easy and it won't be fast, but if you're both invested in the relationship, you'll find a happy medium both parties can live with for the meantime.

◆ *Reminder.* Keep at the forefront of your mind the reason you two are together despite all the hardships, the distance, the hard work. When you come to the conclusion that it's because you both love each other and want to fight for it, not just about it, you'll know what to do.

Chapter 46

Giving Up on Long Distance Love

. . . .

Relationships are hard. They take time, effort, hard work, dedication, time. They work when both parties want them to work. They work when both parties *work* for them to work. They can never be one-sided, and they can never be forced. Sooner or later, the truth will always come out, and that truth is sometimes hard to accept.

So you've put in the time, you've paid your dues, you've hung on for a good chunk of time (a freaking year to be exact), and you expect the payout. Now it seems like all you do is fight, all you do is reproach, all you do is roll your eyes at the guy on the Skype call for the third time in as many minutes. You're both at your wits end. It's coming crashing down, and you can feel it in every fiber of your being. Even things he says are irritating now. He used to be so fun, and now can't seem to breathe without causing you to roll your eyes, or irritate you.

Why does he have to breathe like that? Jeez, goddamnit, fuck. Why can't he just breathe like a normal person? And why the hell does he have to wear that stupid ass sweatshirt? It's so damn hot here in Las Vegas, a million miles away, and he's wearing a freaking sweatshirt. Fucking Montana and it's cool weather. Fuck it all. To hell.

You feel yourself giving up. You don't want to, but it's happening. It's happening without your consent. You can't stop it, and you don't even know how. All you know is that the check-out guy at WholeFoods looked at you kinda funny and he smiled more than usual and now you have that in your mind and your long distance boo is sorta kinda getting in the way. And he's irritating, and annoying now. More than ever.

So what do you do? You have a potentially fun, exciting new adventure with that cute guy at WholeFoods and you can feel it in your veins. You're ready for some body on body action. The possibility has you practically drooling.

It's time to give it a break. Or break it off completely.

Chapter 47

Take a Minute and Breathe, or a Week

....

Sometimes radio silence does a body good. Like really, really good. Ridiculously good. Sometimes all it takes to realize what you had (and still have) was good, is some time to yourself. Or some time with your girls and their horror dating stories. Or some time meeting a few fuckboys and bam! You're cured.

So, all of a sudden you realize you had it good all along. Sure, your boo is far, far away, but he loves you. He accepts you. He respects you. He genuinely wants the best for you. You, on the other hand, love him too. Not just love him, you're in love with him, and yes, you even love the bad too.

The week (or weeks) alone has proven that much. You miss him and you want him back. It's not like you two called it quits. Not really, anyway. All you said is you needed some time, and he agreed. He needed time, too. It was getting to be too much too soon and too far. So you're cured. Now what?

Making the first move is always scary, but it's also incredibly ballsy. It's taking what you want and owning it. Put all your fears, pride, worries away and just do it. Start simple, start friendly, start easy just like you both once were. Say something like, "*Sooo, I just went to the strip with my girls, and guess what I had?*" and add a picture of that ridiculously large Eiffel Tower alcoholic slushy he was having when you two first met. Make it easy to follow up with, take it easy, start a light convo, find something of interest to both of you.

Don't—by all that you love—start off where you left off. I mean, don't say something like, "*So, how was it with that nasty hoe you chatted with a few weeks ago? Ready to come to mama?*" or something equally aggressive. That will not end well. Trust me.

Instead try going soft, loving, caring. Try to start with something of mutual interest. Like that picture you took more than a few weeks ago of the boxers with the words The Best Cock in the World and a picture of a rooster. Tell him it reminded you of him, something cute, something funny, something that will get the convo going. You know your boo! You've been talking for a while, fighting for some too. Take a chance and start it up. He'll not only feel glad you ended the radio silence, but he'll also feel missed and loved.

Sometimes you get lucky and your boo makes the first move. Whatever the reason, they've reached out to you. There's your chance! If you're really missing your boo, don't let a little pride get in the way. Say what you mean and mean what you say. It's really that simple. Go for what you want, and if it's your boo you want, forget all the fights all the things said, and start anew. Sometimes we all say things we don't mean in the heat of a moment that defines our relationship, but does it have to be like that? Evaluate why you asked for a break, how you're feeling and go with your heart.

Chapter 48

Accepting Apologies Like the Goddess You Are

....

Boyfriends can be stupid as hell. Girlfriends, too. Sometimes your boo can be so freaking hard headed that you have to hang up, or end that Skype call, or just stop picking up the phone in general because they've taken it too far.

He's made fun of your pet armadillo (again) and you've had it. So you have an armadillo pet, so freaking what? It was a freaking mistake, jeezzzzz. Now you're stuck with the little critter until he croaks, and you've come to terms with it. But he didn't get it, he's never understood, and now he's hit a nerve. Or a few. He's also made fun of your morning hair-bun for the last time, even though he says it's a joke, it hits a nerve because you're self conscious of your morning hair, like duh. You tame it, but no, it has a mind of it's own. Plus, the only thing you make fun of is his stupid Packers sweatshirt, and damn, with reason. It's old as hell, way oversized, and the letters are peeling on the sides, but nooo you can't make fun of it without him making a big deal out of it. You contemplate bringing up the fact he has a degree he's not even using, but you refrain. You've just made it out of a big problem-hole, and don't want to start a new one. You know he's self conscious of that degree that's just sitting pretty. But still.

He's taken it a little too far, your feelings are hurt, and now he's apologizing. What now? You've already taken a break but it seems like the problems just keep piling on. Maybe you need to visit, but no. No way. You visited last. It's his turn and he can't get time off work until next month because blah blah blah. You're way overdue for a little body heat, and it's showing in your reactions. Now he's calling you back for the third time, and you pick up because you want to hear his voice, but dammit, you're still pissed.

Your boo starts talking and the first thing out of his mouth is "I'm sorry," and you sigh. That's what you wanted to hear. That's what you needed to hear. You take it, and you deserve it.

- *Hot Tip*: When your boo has taken it too far and he's apologizing, take it. Accept the apology like the goddess you are because at the very least he's realized his mistake, and hopefully he's learned. Remember that it's all a learning experience. Next time he'll think twice before making fun of your pet armadillo or that morning bun you're starting to love.

- *Quick Tip*: We all know those people who can't stop bringing up things that happened in the past. Do yourself (and everyone around you) a favor and don't be that person. If you were wronged and accepted an apology, be graceful and don't bring it up. Move on and find other things that piss you off to complain about. If your boo is of flesh and blood, you won't have to wait for long.

Chapter 49

Rejecting and Rejoicing: Not Accepting the Apology

....

Did I mention boyfriends can be stupid as hell? Girlfriends are not exempt, either. People in general can be so freaking stupid. Especially when he has a good thing, he's bound to mess up one way or another. The beautiful thing about this little fact is that most of the offenses are things that offend, but not completely kill a relationship. Unless that no good a-hole has done it this time.

It's entirely your prerogative to accept or reject an apology. Depending on your moral ground and the crime committed, some offenses are better off forgotten, and some warrant a complete shut off.

Consider infidelity, for example. If you find yourself in that situation, whether your boo is the offender or you are, look deep within yourself and find what your moral grounds are. For many, infidelity is the ultimate slap in the face, the definite trust killer and the hole that cannot be climbed out of. The action has been done, does the reason really matter?

It can be anything from feeling lonely (even though you have someone back in another state or country or wherever), to being horny and reckless to wanting to test the waters one toe at a time. Whatever the reason, the deed was done.

Depending on what kind of relationship you have (open to seeing others during the interim or not), infidelity may be a huge deal breaker. Nowadays we see so much infidelity in Hollywood, social media, movies, shows that it can be confusing what we truly believe in.

There are people like Tiger Woods who's wife divorced him for infidelity, and then there's Gabrielle Union who was able to see past the transgression. It all really depends on what you can live with or not.

- *Hot Tip*: If you find that the offense was greater than the relationship, don't feel bad about ending it. Don't fall into the *what if* the world, or your soon to be ex will impose upon you, don't fear the loneliness that comes with being newly single (been there done that and survived). When you know yourself, you'll know the answer and it will be easy to follow it because it will come naturally. All else will fall into place.

- *Cheaters and Cheatees*: Let's take a look at those who didn't take *no crap from no one*.

- Nick Young and Iggy Azalea: The Los Angeles Lakers basketball player was caught on video admitting to cheating on the Aussie rapper. She ended their engagement in June of 2016, showing her standard and keeping to her morals.

- Gavin Rosedale and Gwen Stefani: Not even the beautiful and talented Gwen Stefani could get away from the cheating bug in Hollywood. Gavin Rosedale cheated with their nanny (because he's a dumbass) and when the *Just a Girl* singer found out, she dropped him like a hot tamale, hooked up with country's good boy, Blake Shelton, and had herself a merry good time.

- Tony Parker and Eva Longoria: Another cheater, another athlete, another divorce. Professional basketball player, Tony Parker, cheated on then wife, Eva Longoria, with another team plater's former wife! Yikes! She found out and kicked him to the curb. Now she's married to Jose Antonio Bastón, and if his immense success as president of Televisa, the largest media company in Latin America, doesn't impress, then say his name again. 'Cuz, damn if it isn't sexy as hell.

- Brad Pitt and Jennifer Aniston: We all know this one. Brad left Jen for Angelina and now it's all gone to shit. Karma will fuck you up, even if you're Brad fucking Pitt.

- Kristen Stewart and Robert Pattinson: While men mostly take the cheating cake, that's not to say some women aren't cheating crap, too. Take Kristen Stewart who broke tween's hearts all over the world when it was found out she cheated on Rob with the director of Snow White and the Huntsman in 2012, collectively breaking hearts worldwide including that of Robert Pattinson. She had the vampire, damn. But she had to go fuck it up.

- *Reminder*: Cheating sucks whether you're famous or not. So, set your standards, let them be known, and stick to them.

Chapter 50

Take Another Breather
Because, How Many do You Need?

....

So, it wasn't a cardinal sin, it wasn't even a sin. He just got on your nerves one too many times and you're ready for another break. It's only been a few weeks since the last time this happened and it's starting to feel like a pattern. It's just a break because you need it.

Or maybe it's that the bartender from that dive bar you frequent has started making googly eyes at you and now you have to see where that takes you even though you know bartenders are costumer service workers and their job is literally to be nice to you. So there you go again.

It'll probably be just a couple of weeks before you realize what you kinda sorta maybe already know, but you have to make sure. So you take another break, and dammit, this better be the last one.

Chapter 51

Summer is the Worst

································

Ahh, summer.

Beaches, chlorine filled pools, concerts by the pool, beach balls, bikinis, speedos —the whole bit. It's a wonderful time to be alive; the sun on your face, that perfect tan, cocktails by the pool, fruit platters. Everything is better in the summer. Everything is bright and full of life.

It's just wonderful.

It's also a wonderful time for break-ups. It's a time when people just want to have fun, and if that means dropping their hot tamale who likes to sit and watch Netflix while eating chips every other day instead of said concerts by the pool, then so be it. It may be hard for like two weeks, it may even hurt, but it must be done.

No one wants their boo to lick their cheese-powdered fingers more than they lick them, I'm just saying. It's a fact of life. And that's in person!

It's even harder to stay afloat if your relationship suffers distance woes. So unless you're planning to travel a lot during the summer or take in your tourist boo for even weeks at a time, plan on some friction happening, if not entirely breaking up. Not all relationships fail, not even during the summer, but temptation is always there, lurking in the blades of grass or bubbling up in your mimosa.

It sucks when you meet your soulmate and he's miles away. Like thousands of miles away. I'm not talking the 45-minute drive from Henderson to Summerlin, I'm talking real distance. It sucks even more when both of you have jobs to upkeep and can't just run off to loveland every time you're feeling a little lonely, a little frisky, or a little unsure.

Summertime is just another time to work hard at keeping your relationship untouchable, but if it's just one of you working hard, then you my dear, are fucked. Getting on the same page is easier said than done. Your boo may be saying one thing and doing another, or you may be saying one thing while eyeing another.

- ◆ *Hot Tip*: You're going to need a lot or work, and that work comes in three forms: communication, trust, and the mythical compromise. It may be scary to wear your feelings on your sleeve, but if you want to survive a relationship that may be sinking, or even one on the rocks, there is nothing better than honesty to get you by. Even if your relationship is peachy keen, honesty is the way to go. And if there's one thing honesty does, it's create a bridge to communication.
- ◆ Look here, if you're not afraid to "slob the knob" or "lick the pussycat," or whatever you want to call it (every single one of you understood and don't pretend you didn't), how in the hell are you going to be afraid of voicing your concerns, fears, wants, desires, and goals to your significant other? Be more

afraid of misunderstandings, be more self conscious of mistrust that may happen if you don't speak up. Be cautious of missed compromises, but don't be afraid to speak your mind, and definitely don't be afraid to listen. It goes both ways, and if your boo isn't getting it, have them read this book, jeez.

- You're welcome.

Chapter 52

Break Up to Make Up

....

Break up to make up, that's all we do
First you love me, then you hate me
That's a game for fools.

Oh, how we love oldies. They're honest and oh, so true and real. They hit those heart strings like no other, and man, are they right. Breaking up to make up is a game for fools.

You heard The Stylistics.

It's a game for fools.

But it's a game the best of us are expert players at. Besides, aren't we all fools in love? You know dammed well you lose your mind, girl. Don't try to fool yourself. It's a game too many couples play, and one that can be addictive with the stratospheric highs and the hellish lows.

You like drama and strong emotions, your boo likes to bring up his ex—the mother of his child—a few more times than you would like. You act on it, you lose your mind. He says it's nothing, it's just that she's on his mind because of court. He has you, after all. He loves you. Wants you. You remind him he'll lose a good thing if he loses you. Weeks pass, and there it is again. He brings her up. And you lose it for the last time. Your penchant for drama takes over and you scream and shout and fight and that's that.

It's summer, after all, and you have your eyes on that lifeguard at the Cosmopolitan pool. He's cute and tan and you can bet he's not into talking about his ex. So you break it off, but this time it's feeling a little more permanent than the last few times.

You decide to ask that lifeguard for his number. What's a summer without a fling, anyway?

Chapter 53

Summer is Over, Now What?

....

Summer is almost on it's last leg. School is starting again, the weather is cooling, and the pools are closing. You haven't talked to your boo (because in your mind he's still your boo) for over a month, and you're missing him more than ever.

You're holding out. You kinda sorta can't believe he hasn't texted you by now. Not a single call. Not even a drunken text. Nada. You've come close to calling. You've almost hit the dial button, but you haven't.

Poolboy turned out to be yet another dud, but even so, you've been strong.

The memory of your boo bringing up his ex is still an issue for you. Maybe they're married by now, you really don't know. You've been staying alive with margaritas and tacos at midnight. It's really not healthy but you've enjoyed your time of reflection. Even though you're stubborn, you want to talk to your boo every day a little more.

Then one day he calls you. He says he misses you. Tells you, "*if we could start anew, I wouldn't hesitate. I'd gladly take you back, and tempt the hand of fate. Tears on my pillow, pain in my heart, caused by you,*" and you laugh and tell him that's just a song. An oldie but a goody. You remember why you love him so much. Why it doesn't work out with someone else even when it's not working with him. Because the worst times with him are better than the best times with someone else.

Chapter 54

To Break Up or Not to Break Up: That is the Answer

....

here comes a time when the possibility of breaking up is so tangible, you have to think
the likelihood. More than that, you analyze it. Love can't be measured and it can't be
eighed. There's no scientific formula for love. It's chemicals in the brain, it's cupid's
row, it's the tides of the sea, it's the facets of the moon. Love fades. Love changes.
ou can analyze the crap out of love and your feelings and the possibility of a break up,
ut when there are leftover feelings, the process is almost impossible. Letting go of
omeone that needs letting go of is the hardest thing to do.

It's not news your boo is not perfect. It's pretty fucking obvious by now, actually.
e's annoying, and moody, and likes to play video games more than your twelve year
d neighbor. He drinks domestic beer (eww), and has no idea what Chardonnay even
. He wears Green Bay Packers sweatshirts year-round, and eats cereal for dinner.
e's childish, and tacky. His favorite food is taco pizza, and his idea of cooking is
rowing together boxed mac and cheese. He thinks you own too much makeup and
ou spend too much time on your eyebrows. He's needy and greedy, sensitive and
oprehensive, he refuses to kill spiders and cries a lot, he loses weight abnormally fast
nd gains muscle slow as a snail. He listens to bad music and watches movies a
ousand times over. He's silly and cute. He's caring and loving. He's smart and funny
nd giving. He's the best and the worst, the coolest and the nerdiest, he's so much. He
ves freely and openly and it takes you by surprise sometimes how honest he is. He
uys you makeup, even though he says you have too much, he spoils you, he calls you
nd texts you and lets you have your girls night out without complaint, he carries your
urse when you're together, he visits more than you visit him, he makes you feel loved
nd cared about and cared for.

He's the best and he's the worst.

You make a pro/con list and the list grows and grows, the cons build up, the pros
dd on too. It's confusing because you know you love him but you feel there's
omething missing. It's confusing because you love him and you adore him, but you
so hate him for being so far away.

You write and write your thoughts away. You contemplate, you cry, you get angry
nd break five mugs, but it's better the mugs than your phone. The anger engulfs you, it
ecomes you. And finally, after all that analyzing, after all that writing, after all the anger,
hits you.

The problem is the distance. It's shopping alone around a million couples. It's
ating ice cream alone next to hand-holding teenagers. It's all your friends getting
ngaged, it's the lonely nights and the third-wheeling you've been doing. It's the being
one, yet not. It's the relationship you have with your phone. It's all of it.

Chapter 55

Confusion at its Best

You've figured out the bug that's been making you moody. It's the little creeping feeling that this, what you both have, will always be a never-ending long distance relationship, that you two will never be what you really want to be: a close-distance couple, and in your eyes, a real couple. The kind of couple that does things, sexy and not so much, goes places, meets friends and parents and coworkers. A real-world relationship. The realization has you moping around and it's mainly because you're so fucking confused about everything involving him, and everything you've done the past year.

You allowed it all to happen, so who are you, really? What did you get yourself into? You knew this relationship would be hard the minute he called telling you he'd made the decision to leave. You knew he would be far away. You knew it all. You could've made your decision then to drop it while you could. But you didn't. And now you want more. You're ready for more, and you can't believe he's not, that he's content where he's at, where your relationship has unfolded to. And that right there, knowing he's okay with you here and him there, hurts more than you'd like to admit.

You do as you're told. You talk to your boo, you *communicate*, yet nothing changes. He won't leave, he won't move, he won't come back.

But he's not the only one who can move. You can, too. And you think about it, try to imagine your life in a little cute Montana town with your boo, but in the end, you can't. The idea of living in that tiny apartment, with him away most of the time at work or at court or in meetings gets to you. It's not like you're a fucking child who needs constant supervision, but you do need companionship. That's what you're crying out for. And maybe, just maybe he's not the one who can give you what you need.

So you're at a quandary: break up and start anew or stay feeling unsure and unaccomplished.

- *Hot Tip*: If you are feeling like the previous paragraphs, be honest with yourself. We all know being single sucks like hell, but being in an unsatisfying relationship can be even worse.
- If it's not working for you, let it go! Be the goddess you know you are, put on your big girl panties, and go for what you want. If it's freedom to start anew, by all means.
- It it's fighting for what you already have, evaluate how much effort your partner is giving and be direct. Ask him what he really wants. Don't be afraid of the answer. More than likely, whatever the answer is, it will set you free. Free of confusion, free of the fear of failure, free of the what-ifs.
- If he wants to call it quits, at the very least you know you've done your duty. You've done all you could and your sideways feelings were on to something.

- If he wants to work it out, girl you got this! Do the hard work, reap the benefits.

Chapter 56

Ghosting and What Happens Next

....

So you've been contemplating things lately, and you hope it all turns around for the better. Your spirits are high, your laugh is loud, your happiness is contagious. Life is great, so of course something has to go wrong.

Like, so fucking wrong.

The nightly calls have seemed to stop. You call but instead of the usual hello you hear after the first ring, it keeps ringing until it goes to voicemail. Your calls go unanswered, your texts unread, your voicemails unreturned. You're feeling left out, abandoned.

It's so not like him. You contemplate calling all the Montana hospitals, his parents, his neighbors, his friends but you don't. Instead you go on Instagram and he's active. He's posted a picture of him playing Black Ops, cereal on the coffee table as usual, headset and all.

You let it go, pour a glass of rosé, read *#GirlBoss*, and go to bed. That nagging feeling is in your chest, but you stifle it. Tomorrow will be better. But tomorrow comes and it's not. And your call goes to voicemail again.

This time, not even *#GirlBoss* can help.

- *Hot Tip*: Unfortunate are those guys who just stop calling. Ghosting, is it? More like a freaking premonition of their future selves. Screw stabbing him with a fork, this time the stabbing will be in the soul—with a poison-laden hatchet. They'll be a fucking ghost for ghosting a goddess, that's for sure. Trust.
- I'm not sure where this ghosting thing started, but it's a real dick move. It must be something about millennials and our flare for the dramatic or our sense of entitlement. Otherwise, what can possibly persuade you to just stop talking? The most immature fucking move out there, if you ask me.
- If you find yourself in this situation, there is only one thing to do. Move on, hunty. Move on so fucking much that the great Sophia Amoruso will be looking up to you for advice and inspiration.
- Take up hobbies, go to concerts, go places you usually don't, go skydiving, stay busy, be yourself again. We all know we lose just a bit of ourselves when we star a new relationship and that can be even worse when it's been as long as a year. So take the time to find yourself again, do things that make you happy. You'll meet new people, open yourself to opportunities to meet a real flesh and blood guy.

- *Quick Tip*: Live and life will happen. It's really that simple. It's my favorite advice to give.

Chapter 57

What if You Stop Calling?

....

As explained above, ghosting is not cool here, in China or Mars. So do the world a favor and just don't do it!

Ghosting is for pussies with no backbone. It's for people who don't have the courage to stand up for what they believe in and for what they want. It's not cool to leave anything open ended like that. It just isn't.

So put on your big girl panties, take a doubleshot of vodka, and call that a-hole who's making your life miserable. Talk it out. He'll probably cry. You'll feel really bad. It will pull your heart strings, it will make you sweat, it will make your eyebrows pinch together and remind you worrying causes wrinkles. Do not give in. Make up your mind and keep it.

Women have this stigma of being fickle, but who the hell isn't when you have a crying man-baby on your hands?

- *Hot Tip*: Honesty and a hard resolution will take you far in this situation. Be honest with yourself, stay hard set on your decision, and remember that breaking up is hard to do.
- You know, you've done it before. Plenty of times, girl, so don't even try to be coy. Keep your eye on the main goal: Getting to know yourself again as a single girl, that cute guy at the gym maybe, or that new Tinder match. Whatever floats your boat.
- It'll be hard for the first few days, but then a freedom will overcome you and you'll know you've made the right choice.

- *Quick Tip*: Yes, this shit is depressing, I know that. If these scenarios don't apply to you and your annoyingly perfect relationship, just skip it! Better yet, read it and feel better about yourself and your peachy keen relationship. Skank.

Chapter 58

When He Complains it's Just Not Enough

······························

Sometimes you're happy as a clam, laughing the days away, feeling the love from your phone to your laptop to your cooch. The sporadic visits are just enough to keep you sated, and those nightly calls keep you on track.

Sure, it would be great to wake up to his stinky morning breath, or to lay your eight pound head on his sparsely hairy chest after a naughty round, or stare at his different colored eyes in the sunset, but here you are. Miles away and happy as ever.

You appreciate the good, see the bad, and pray for the future. It's all cotton candy skies for you. He's sent you a mold of his slightly crooked dick, and though it's not as big as you hoped (just kidding, boo!), you take it. Like forreal.

You keep that after glow all by yourself because you're a fucking adult and you can take care of yourself, thank you very much. Life is good, flowers bloom, and the skies are blue. Everything is great, and love is in the air.

Then your boo blindsides you out of nowhere.

He's not happy. I mean, not really. He wants more. He finds himself wanting more than just those phone calls, more than those Skype moments, more than just a six second Snap of half your tatas. He wants it all. And he wants it all 4D.

He wants you, he wants your smell, your makeup bag, your overflowing closet, your super old boots you refuse to toss, your book collection, even your teddybear collection, he wants it all. He's asked you to move to Montana with him, to ease the pain of being apart. He's even begged. He pretends he's just kidding, but he's serious. Living a thousand miles away is just not enough for him.

He can't move back because he has a good job, he gets paid way better than you do, and his court case is in Montana. Besides, the job market is overflowing with opportunities for you. The hospital is always hiring, at least.

You're seriously fucked, because up until that moment, you thought he would be the one moving back. I mean, who leaves a town of three million people, wonderful restaurants, lively nightlife, and amazing shopping for a podunk town in Montana? Who? No one, that's who. No one except your freaking boyfriend. But still. Montana has never, ever been on your radar. You can't even point to it in a map. You've been to Yellowstone, but he says there's more to Montana than that. He even mentions Flathead Lake and all the rich people that live there. He's trying to get your attention. He's trying to sound alluring and great, amazing and different. There's hiking, he says. And snowboarding, and lakes and rivers and wildlife and it's starting to sound fantastic until he says there's hunting and fishing.

Then you wonder what the hell you'd do in a hunting town when you're a freaking vegetarian.

So you decide that you can't move. At least not yet. The idea hasn't been entirely formed in your mind because you can't imagine living there. You'd probably die.

And so he says it's just not enough for him. He needs more than just phone and FaceTime calls, more than Snapchat and Instagram to feel like he's truly doing something, involved in something bigger than just him. It's just not enough.

Far away you is not enough, or at least that's all you hear.

Chapter 59

When to Let it Go

....

It's been a back and forth rollercoaster, a merry-go-round of crap that just gets tossed around and not fixed. You refuse to move, so does he. It's an impasse, and a pretty fucking horrible one at that. You're both stubborn as shit and you're left feeling unappreciated, undervalued, and unloved.

Not too long ago you could make a man do whatever you wanted with just the mention of your cooch, but this sucker is proving to be more difficult than that. It doesn't help he has a son to worry about, so your cooch takes second place which is a big reason you want to end it all. You need to be numero uno, and he's not delivering.

You tell yourself that if it wasn't for the little cutie pie, you'd have your boo eating from the palm of your hand, or licking candy off of your vagina, but still.

Everyday that passes is another reminder that you're not alone yet you're not together. It's a cold way to live, and a fucked up way to relationship (yes, I used that as a verb. Sue me). It's becoming more and more clear that it's time to let it all go to shit. It's a thread away from it anyway. The love has turned to spite. Attraction has turned to annoyance. Respect has turned to nagging. It's all crap, and you both know it.

The nightly calls still happen, though shorter and shorter every day. You say something snippy, he sighs and says he has to shower, he snaps at your singing, you suddenly have to wash your hair, you call him out on his little accent, he all of a sudden has to run to the store for more shaving cream. It's all crumbling down and you can't stop it.

It's becoming clearer and clearer: a breakup is inevitable.

Chapter 60

How to Let it Go

....

When the decision has been made to let a relationship go, there's only one sure way to do it. And that's to stop it cold turkey. Cut all forms of communication. Block if you must. Just do it. It's going to hurt, I know. It's going to suck, and you're probably going to gain ten pounds in ice cream alone, but in the end it will be the right thing to do.

You may want to start a fight, go lurking for evidence, argue about something to give you fuel to finally do it, but it's not needed. It's even better if you just go out and say it. You're not happy. You want more. It's not enough. You've met someone else. Whatever the reason, be honest. Don't go with clichés like "it's not you it's me," we all know that one and we all know it's bull. Instead just stand up for what you want and do it.

- *Hot Tip*: Breaking up is hard to do. So much so, there are millions of songs on the matter, movies, novels, musicals, the whole bit. So if you're in need of some glutton for punishment, here are some of my absolute favorite movie tear jerkers.

    I.   Eternal Sunshine for the Spotless Mind
    II. (500) Days of Summer
    III. Blue Valentine
    IV. Nights in Rodanthe (because you hate yourself, that's why)
    V.   The Vow
    VI. Pride and Prejudice (the 2004 version, because Mr. Darcy, duh)
    VII. A Walk to Remember
    VIII. Like Crazy
    IX. The Notebook
    X.   Titanic (because, fuck it)
    XI. The Great Gatsby
    XII. Pearl Harbor
    XIII. My Girl

- When you're done emptying your Kleenex box and are ready for some lighthearted fun, try these:

    I.   My Best Friend's Wedding
    II. Forgetting Sarah Marshall
    III. The Break-up
    IV. Bridesmaids
    V.   The First Wives Club

VI.   Blood in Blood Out (because yes, that's why)
VII. Dirty Dancing
VIII. Bridget Jones' Diary (all of them)
IX.   He's Just Not That Into You
X.   How to Lose a Guy in Ten Days
XI.   Ten Things I Hate About You
XII. Heathers
XIII. Deathproof
XIV. Kill Bill

♦   *Reminder*: Whatever your mood, press play on that sucker, pop some corn and sit tight. It'll be over soon. I promise.

Chapter 61

Watch a Fuckload of Crime Shows

....

This little tidbit might be my best advice of all freaking time. If you're still feeling like you miss the crap out of that sucker who left you for Montana, then consider watching some good old fashioned crime shows. Nothing like a little crime to get your mind out of the gutter.

My ultimate favorites are as follows:

   I.   Snapped
   II.   Women Who Kill
   III.   Wives with Knives
   IV.   Deadly Women
   V.   Fatal Attraction
   VI.   Killer Women, etc.

Basically anything where a woman kills the problem, or problems in her life. It's not psycho, it's preventative. Trust me, watching all these women kill the men in their lives because they couldn't say *hasta la vista, baby* will sober you up in no time. Especially after the sentencing. Who wants to spend the best years of her life behind bars all for a no-bit, good for nothing a-hole who would've been a has-been in her fabulous life? That's right. No one.

So get that popcorn popping, prop your feet up, get that cozy blanket, and watch away, my friend. No one is judging.

Chapter 62

When the Bloodbath
is Finished and You Miss The One

....

Relationships are freaking hard, and decisions can change. Have I said women are fickle? Many men are too, don't fall for that little piece of misinformation. Women get blamed for it all, but trust, guys can be hormonal, fickle, emotional and the whole bit.

It can sometimes come as a surprise to know that you want your old fling back. It can also seem fickle, even to you. Especially after dipping your toes in the potential mate pool. Duds, idiots, misogynists, and the like will have you changing your mind quite quickly. It doesn't help you need a few failures before knowing a good thing when you see one. Or knowing you let one go for a winded caprice.

You thought you wanted flesh, you thought you wanted dates and car rides, and dinners and bubble baths, morning sex and foot rubs, lazy nights in and laughing in the middle of the night, but you forgot a crucial piece. You forgot you needed to love a man so much, so fully, so honestly that you *wanted* to do all those things with him, experience all those things and more. It's become apparent not just anyone will do. And you find yourself missing your boo more than ever.

What you got on your time of experimentation were half-smart idiots with split tongues and brainless hard bodies with too much powdered protein instead of the connection and undeniable love you were looking for.

You miss your boo, the one with the different colored eyes, the one with the smile and the lips. The one who makes you smile and fills your heart with joy. The one who calls without fail and loves you like crazy. You miss your boo, because he's The One.

It's taken you disappointments, heartbreak, dissolution, a series of bad dates, fear and pain, longing and distance, but you finally know. He's The One. You love him. You miss him. And you want him back.

Chapter 63

Getting Back Together

....

You've broken up and gotten back together more than a few times. You've taken him for granted and he's seen your crazy side more than you'd like to admit. He's still far, far away, and you're still not ready to move to a small town in Montana with no Best Buy. But you miss your boo and you want him back. So you text him, something cute, something inconspicuous.

It's been a few months, and you don't know if a stupid skank has him eating out of her palm (eww, gross visual), but you try anyway. He responds quicker than you imagined. You thought maybe he would let you sweat it out, but he's not like that. Never has been. So he answers pretty quickly, and in that same witty manner you're so used to yet so distant from.

You flirt, you device plans, you get a strategy. He'll be yours again if it kills you. Luckily it doesn't have to, because he tells you he misses you. He hasn't fallen for anyone the way he did for you in a long time, and is not sure he ever will again. Your heart dances, it makes pirouettes, it freaking almost beats out of your chest. He confesses he's been miserable without you, and it's the best thing you've heard in months. You tell him you miss him too. That you'll take him even as a friend because he means so much to you.

He asks you to be his girlfriend again. That this time, he will tell you how much he loves you and show you too. That he'll do anything possible to be everything you want from him, and you tell him he already is. That you love him and miss him and want him back. And you both promise to be the best you can, give it your all, and not let a little distance get in the way.

You're more in love than ever.

Chapter 64

Doing Cute Shit Because that's What's Holding this Together

....

It's back to cute pet names and naked selfies and it's better than ever. He's kept his word. He's working hard to be there for you, even on the days he has to work extra hours.

His efforts are not going unnoticed.

You're calling more, you're doing cute shit and you're liking it all. It's all morning calls while brushing your teeth, and wishing him a great day at work. It's him calling during his lunch hour just to let you know he's thinking of you. It's watching movies together, miles apart, but feeling like you're together. It's midnight phone calls when you wake up from a nightmare and he comforts you back to sleep. It's receiving a surprise gift from him, and when you open it it's Jeffree Star highlighters—the ones you told him about three weeks ago when you found out they'd be in stock two weeks later and he shows you he's there, he's listening, he cares, he's trying.

He tells you about his favorite childhood book and you spot it at Target and you send it to him with a cute note telling him you love him more than ever. That you can't wait to be together. That you appreciate everything he does for you. That you love him for who he is.

It's all the cute shit you can take, but you love it.

You love it and you're proud.

Chapter 65

Send Him a Sweatshirt of a Picture of Your Face by Mail Yes, Snail Mail!

....

Scrolling through Instagram is nothing short of torture sometimes. Beautiful people, crazy fit bodies, amazing vacations, impeccable makeup skills—exactly nothing you have but yet you're there like a voyeuristic masochist.

Rare are the times when you find something that truly speaks to your soul, something so genius, so *you*, that you have to have it. Or better said, your better half has to have it.

That's when you decide to send him a sweatshirt he can proudly wear all year round, a sweatshirt that won't be an obnoxious shade of yellow, and one he will no doubt love: Your face.

That's right.

You've found a website that will make any piece of clothing or mug or mousepad with any picture you choose. And you've chosen yourself, or better said, a picture of your beautiful face plastered on a nice shade of gray sweatshirt. It's the best thing you've thought of in forever. And when you send it, a little tingling of excitement starts in your belly and doesn't go away.

When he gets his surprise he sends you a picture of your gift with a huge smile on his face. At night, he sends you a picture of your sweatshirt on a pillow and he's kissing it.

It's the cutest shit you've seen in forever. And that tingling in your belly has suddenly moved down to your cooch. You can't wait for him to visit, and it's all because of that cute shit you've been doing.

Thank snail mail. It's a godsend when you're being coy.

- ◆ *Hot Tip*: Long distance relationships can be super hard, so enjoying everything you're dealt is sometimes hard, but consider using those hardships to your advantage.
- ◆ Send him cute gifts, surprise him with pizza one day, send your girl her favorite band's new vinyl for her favorite turntable, make it a tradition to send cute things that remind you of him and make it a surprise.
- ◆ Little things like that make your boo feel included, important and safe in the relationship.
- ◆ On the flip side, they'll reinforce the love you both have for each other and keep that hint of playfulness and surprise alive during those times when visiting is not an option.

Chapter 66

Surprise!

....

There are few things in life more worthwhile than seeing your boo surprised. That initial shock, that startled look, the look of disbelief, then that crazy laugh, then understanding, then confusion—it's like music to your eyes. Beautiful music you've created. And all it took was a few clicks of the mouse, a couple of hours on a plane, and ingenuity sneaking into his apartment.

That's right.

You've surprised him with a visit. It's Friday and he has the whole weekend to bullshit, and he's going to do it with you. As far as he knows you're in Las Vegas (or wherever), planning on having a quiet weekend, mostly watching movies and drinking wine while talking to your boo on the phone. It's your favorite pastime and his, too.

But you remember him saying something about the way his doorhandles jiggles because of that one time he broke into his own apartment after forgetting his keys. He mentions a credit card will do the trick every time. He considers changing the handle just to be safer, but before he has the chance, you take flight and surprise him.

You take a shower to be fresh and put on your favorite pair of jeans and top, your cute shit. You sit on the sofa and wait for him to arrive with anticipation that's killing you. Every sound makes your heart beat faster, every car door shutting makes you sweat a little bit more, every footstep has your heart on your throat. Your stomach feels like it's permanently stuck on the drop of a rollercoaster, and it's beautiful.

It's as exciting for you as it will be surprising for him.

When the door finally opens you lose it and laugh like crazy. He's shocked, his eyes widen, he drops everything and runs to you, picks you up and twirls you around a few times.

It's the best decision you've ever made. Just the look in his different colored eyes is worth it.

Then he kisses you, he hugs you, he tugs you, he squeezes you and then, after a few minutes of laughing and kissing and trying to figure it out, he takes you to his bedroom and all of a sudden all the doubts leave your mind and you have the best sex of your life.

- ◆ *Hot Tip*: Don't be afraid to let go and act on your crazy ideas! Your boo will appreciate it as much as you're going to enjoy doing it. At the end of the day, it'll be one more story to tell, one more adventure to live, so let go and live a little.
- ◆ When you prioritize fun in a relationship it is heightened to a new level. A level that's alluring, addictive, and so much fun.

- *Quick Tip*: Don't get shot! Know your partner. If he or she will get freaked out by this ingenious surprise, and has a gun handy, don't do it!

Chapter 67

Work, Work, Work, Work, Work: Because Rhianna Got it Right it Takes Work to Make it Work

....

Your relationship has made huge progress and it's better than ever, but just because it's on a high does not mean you two can stop working at it. People experience highs and lows in life just as in relationships and living on a high can lead to trouble when the lows come because the standard has been set. Don't plan on lows but don't be surprised when they come, just keep in mind that all relationships take work, and romantic ones are no exception.

So do like Rhianna and work. Work at making it work, work at making your boo feel loved, work at making your boo feel appreciated, and when a low hits, work at getting past it. It's all about respect and understanding.

So your boo has decided to go on a trip. Yay! That usually means he's coming to see you and you can just see it. The lights, the glitz, the restaurants, the romantic walks at the mall, all the sex you plan on having...all of it. It's your favorite time, after all. It's when you get to see your boo, and have him, too. It's the best.

Then all of a sudden he says he's visiting his parents and his cousin who just had a baby for the third time and you go deaf. You can't hear him past all the blood rushing to your face in anger and disbelief.

How could he prefer to see his family, the one he *grew up with* than see you, his freaking girlfriend who gives him love and attention and amazing sex? The old you would've lost it. Would've made a scene to the end of the world, but the new you is different. You think things through this time. You tell him it's his choice, that you're a little disappointed, a little sad, but that you support him.

He says he was afraid to tell you because he was afraid you would act out, afraid you would be so mad you'd end it again. But no, not this time. It's all about compromises anyway. He's visited you after your surprise visit, and more than once. It's more frequent than before and that's what has you expecting another visit. It's too long without him if it goes over a couple of weeks without seeing your boo. But you digress. You tell him to have fun and not forget you. He laughs and says he'll text you every hour on the hour. And he does.

Maybe your boo accidentally FaceTimes you and you look cute as hell so you answer even though it wasn't a planned FaceTime call but he's not paying attention. He's butt dialed you and you hear him talking to that brunette you know is his neighbor. The one that gave you a funny look when you were breaking into his apartment but you thought you'd found a true playa sister because the cops never showed.

You know it's her because of that high pitched voice she has and though you take a deep breath before jumping to conclusions you clearly hear her ask if he has a cigarette. He says no because he quit (under your command, but still). She laughs and says oh, yes, she remembers. He quit. She starts making conversation but he cuts her off, telling her he has to make it to a meeting. Good boy.

When he realizes what's been happening he backtracks, he says it was just a coincidence she was there, he *swears*. But you know all this because you heard it all. And you tell him you believe him, that you trust him. Because that's what couples who are in love do. They trust. He smiles and says he really has that meeting to get to, his eyes full of love and appreciation for your understanding.

That's the work it takes to make it work. It takes trust and a heavy hand of it, too. He never has to know you heard it all. All he has to know is that you believe him.

Ta da! Making it work is freaking easy.

- *Hot Tip*: If your boo suddenly decides to visit his family for his next trip instead of you, don't lose your shit. Relax and find some common ground. Remember that this is all part of making it work. You can't be the only one in his life, though you may want to be.
- Be confident enough to know that you're his girl, and he's your guy. Be confident enough to know that just because he's traveling somewhere else, he doesn't still want to be with you. Be confident enough to know that your boo or you can be somewhere else in the world and your relationship is strong enough to withhold, that your bond is and always will be there. Be confident enough to know that some extra distance will change nothing (unless that distance is closed, because sex, duh).
- Making it work is compromising, it's giving and taking, it's finding a happy balance that works. So don't make everything about yourself, and don't make everything about your boo. Find that happy balance and live it.

Chapter 68

Something's Gotta Give

....

You've been together now for quite a while. It seems that it's been forever because all that you've gone through, all that you've survived. It's been a rollercoaster of emotions and wave after wave of ups and downs. You've reached your boiling point with the distance more than once, and now it's time to close that distance gap. Something's gotta give and if it doesn't soon, you might lose it again.

It doesn't help that your boo is freaking hot and his neighbors are girls and cute girls at that, and the more time that passes the more thought you give it and you can feel those little insecurities starting to arise, but you shut them down because you've been there done that. But still.

You want more, and you've been telling yourself that having your boo even from afar is better than nothing but you can feel your resolve starting to explode. Like that smiling volcano in Hawaii, your crazy is just begging to be let out with an evil smile and weird eyes.

Something's gotta give, that much is clear. It's coming up on a year and three months, and the time and distance are getting to you. You tell him about it. It's been bothering him, too, he says. He's been thinking of moving back. His old boss has told him he has a job anytime he decides to return, and he's considering it. His court case is not done, and it's probably going to take longer still, but he can travel back and forth, can't he? And you tell him that you're surprised he's considering moving back since he's been so adamant about his choice to move, but he says he can't take the distance much longer. He wants something concrete with you.

He needs you, and he needs you bad.

Chapter 69

Set a Date and Keep it

....

There comes a time in all long distance relationships when distance just doesn't cut it. The main goal of a long distance relationship is to make it work during the time apart, and eventually—however long it takes—to be together living a maximum of 45-minutes away at the most. Unless you're some freaking celebrity with a crazy schedule and you're dating another celebrity you see every four months, and it won't be changing anytime soon, then whatever floats your boat.

So, for us mere mortals, get excited, plan things out, get your cute Kate Spade planners and your trusty calendars out because it's finally happening! You're going to live in the same city, you're finally going to be together! And man, it feels good to say it out loud. And it feels even better to imagine all the stuff you'll do together. And thinking about all that amazing sex...damn, it's really happening.

Setting the date is so freaking exciting whether you're moving states, or you know, getting married. Whether your boo is moving to you or you're moving to him, the move is as exciting as the other save the date (hint, boo boo, hint).

Take your time, plan out the dates, and get to work. Because moving from apartment to apartment is tough, but moving states—or worse yet, countries—is harder than sneaking into Area 51.

Once your date is set, keep that date. Make your decision and keep it. A lot of work and thought went into deciding the best time, so honor all that work you and your boo have done and keep it.

- *Hot Tip*: Moving can be hard. Really hard. Like so freaking hard you don't want to think about moving for another ten years. To help keep you and your boo on track, keep in mind the end result. Think about why you're doing it, why it matters, and keep your eye on the prize. When you keep your goal on the forefront, all the mishaps and setbacks seem a little less hard to deal with. So, remember to keep your end goal in sight, and give it your all. Because this is the beginning of the rest of your life.

- *Quick Tip*: To make it easier on yourself and your loved one, make sure that the one making the big move has a job lined up to avoid the dreaded unemployment period. Not only will it be easier for you, it will be worlds easier later on when the move takes place and the situating starts.

Chapter 70

The Lucky 30

....

There's nothing particularly lucky about those that stay together to the end—the end being finally being together, not dying, of course.

Those that make it, the 30%, have worked hard and diligently for what they want. Sure, they've had setbacks and more problems than North Korea, but they've overcome them all if not most of them, unlike North Korea.

The lucky ones are really those that have seen failure and hit it upside the head, those that have stayed one step ahead of the breaking-up bug, and gotten the shot for it, too.

Lucky are those who have seen the bad in their partners and still want to bone. Lucky are those who have seen the man of their dreams cry while watching Titanic and have fallen deeper in love. Lucky are those who have survived the distance and the time alone. Lucky are those who have worked past their jealousy and insecurities. Lucky are those that have staved off slutty small town skanks to keep the one they truly love happy, respected and loved. Lucky are those who have kept their vows (a promise of fidelity, of course) to their partner in a small town in Montana while living in party city. Lucky are those who have survived adversity and have seen the light.

You get the picture now.

There's nothing lucky about those 30%.

There's hard work, dedication, sustainable love, passion, and the knowledge that your partner is your home, that together you're not perfect but you are at the same time. No matter what happens, he's your home. Because the way you feel when you're with him is the way you want to feel the rest of your life. They way you feel when you're with him is like you're finally home.

You've made it. You're two of the 30%. You've made it, and you can finally breathe again.

Chapter 71

Moving or Taking in

....

Moving is hard. It is so hard, in fact, most people move on average about 11.7 times during their lifetime according to ACS[4]. I mean, it involves cleaning the crap out of everything you own, tossing, keeping, boxing, taping, labeling, hiring movers or doing it yourself, getting one of those cool Pods, or doing it old school with a Uhaul. It involves goodbye parties at work, and dinner with your girls, tears and drinks and stories and wishes of goodwill, promises to come back and visit them all, threats to have each and every one of them visit you so you don't feel so alone in a new town.

So many things go into moving, that when you're finally there, all you want to do is sleep and rest and eat pizza and drink wine and hope the boxes magically unpack themselves (or that your boo unpacks them for you).

If you are moving in together, there's nothing more important than one little tidbit, one little but important space that can and will break up any relationship if not handled properly: closet space. If you haven't planned ahead of time, your boo will be so freaking surprised to find you own thirty pairs of shoes and twenty jeans and fifteen dresses and a hundred pair of scrubs. So plan ahead, and for all that you love, make sure he knows there is no way in hell you're getting rid of those shoes, or anything you own for that matter, so he better make way. You've already done the hard work and donated loved articles of clothing and let go of that high school skirt you were trying to fit back in. He doesn't want to come between you and your chosen Calvin Klein jeans. Just saying.

If your boo happens to be a man (or woman) who doesn't cook or has seen a proper pan in his life, chances are he's not bringing crap to the kitchen table or owns anything of worth in the kitchen, so feel free to toss what crap he does own and make space for your Giada De Laurentiis cookbooks, and your Rachel Ray cookware. If he cooks, feel free to toss his crap and make way for yours. He'll have much better pans to cook with and a better way to make pasta Fra Diavolo and grilled tofu for you.

- ◆ *Reminder*: Moving does not necessarily mean *moving in*. If you're not ready for that kind of commitment, talk it out. Nothing is better than honesty and transparency. Moving states or countries is commitment enough, and if that's enough for you now, it should be enough for your boo. Time spent together will be exponentially increased anyway, and rushing into things will just create more problems than fix any. So take your time, and enjoy the move!

- ◆ *Hot Tip*: Feeling a little overwhelmed with all the moving boxes? Take a break and watch a movie with your boo, eat dinner, make love, peel potatoes — whatever calms you down. Let go of any anxiety feeling that may be looming over your recent move and what the future may bring and simply enjoy the moment and the new change in your life.

- *Quick Tip*: Getting situated is as important as catching new episodes of The Walking Dead. It's about making a space not just yours, not just your partner's, but making it your own little cocoon of love. Go ahead and christen the whole house, too. Nothing says situated like sex in every nook and cranny. Go crazy. Have fun. Enjoy your move!

Chapter 72

Finding Useful Employment

....

If you planned ahead, hopefully this chapter will be a breeze. Having a job before you move is all around better for your health, your wellbeing, and your nerves. Shop around for job offers in the new town, or help your boo with job postings in your city.

Nothing can tear down a newly moved in (or same city) couple like a few weeks of unemployment can. The lying around in your sweats, the nappy hair, the days without deodorant, the leg hair that has grown extra fast can be a detriment to a newly close relationship. Or maybe your boo is playing Black Ops more than he's searching for a job and his cheese bites are all over the living room floor and his socks haven't been changed for two weeks now (you know because you've been counting), and it's getting on your last nerve so much that you wish he'd just move back to Montana already.

- *Reminder*: To avoid a mishap like this, plan ahead, have a few job interviews lined up and go get them! It will not only keep you happier, but your better half happy as well.

- *Hot Tip*: Making the geographical leap is hard but sometimes it's also necessary. Leaping from job to job can be even harder. So to ease your move, consider virtual job hunting.
- With the age of technology comes the age of ease. So many websites are dedicated to job-hunt that virtually every job available is listed in websites of that sort.
- Websites like indeed.com , monster.com, Job.com, careerbuilder.com, LinkedIn, and many others offer great search options. If you're looking to see what's out there, all you have to do is search.

- *Quick Tip*: Update your curriculum vitae. It's hard to keep up with your resumé and adding every little tidbit you learn and do, but one important thing to keep in mind if you're taking a geographical leap is to change your cover letter.
- Simply state that you're making the move to (blank) city and bam! You're done. Employers can get a little jittery about hiring out of town transplants, but if you state it in your cover letter that you'll be in that new city with or without that job, you're golden. You can try something along the lines of:

Dear Anna,

I will be relocating to Great Falls on August 31, 2016 and the open position at Benefis Hospital is the challenge I am looking for...

Easy peasy.

Chapter 73

Feeling at Home Away From Home

....

It was your lot to relocate, now what? Feeling at home away from home can mean many things. It can be finding restaurants that you love to finding the perfect yoga class to your favorite new bar. It's about getting out there and finding the good that your new city or town or country has to offer.

If it's a different country you find yourself in, getting familiar with the language is a must, getting acquainted with the culture, too.

Any new space needs getting some used to, and as humans, we hate change. If it was your lot in life to relocate, change is just what you need.

Feeling at home can be a simple as having some space just for yourself in the dresser, it can be as simple as having your own drawer for your undies. It can be brushing your teeth while your partner pees. Sometimes feeling at home can mean finding that special place in your new home that makes you feel safe and cuddled. Whether it's the kitchen where you love to cook, or the bathtub where you take your bubble baths, finding that special place is as important as your 30 pairs of shoes and their special place in the closet.

If your boo happens to be an interior designer, I'd suggest going along with his inputs. In fact, do everything your boo says and make your life a little easier. If not, take charge and feel free to toss his juvenile crap out the window. He might as well find out what he's gotten himself into now rather than later.

Find a stupid red fish hanging over your smart TV? Take that crap to the donations box. It's an eye sore and he should know it. Too many video games? Feel free to send a box or two to your cousin in California. He's fifteen and at a much better age for gaming. Your boo should learn that favorites are favorites, and you're not going to put up with a hundred video games in your shared space he has but never plays. Have him choose en he can't live without and get rid of the rest. Growing up is tough, I know. Get over it.

- *Hot Tip*: Moving in is hard! But feeling at home is better than feeling like you've just stepped into some else's life and have to walk on eggshells. Take that first step to clean up his life, because you do it anyway, don't you? Not only will it happen anyway (umm, hello thirty pairs of shoes, goodbye old DVDs he's never going to watch anyway), but taking the first step and easing into it will help. Better you talk about getting rid of his porn stash than him coming back to a home with an empty porn stash which will certainly feel like his days of freedom are over.
- And they are, but we want to ease into in rather than brutally letting him find out. That way he can choose his ultimate favorites and feel like he still has a semblance of who he was before you came into his life and turned it upside down.

- *Quick Tip*: To the less organized or interior design-lacking reading this, if your boo comes in, guns blazing, don't fret! Moving in is hard enough as it is, but losing a part of yourself is completely normal. You're not losing the core of who you are, but merely the bachelor/bachelorette that lives in you.
- Trust in the process, trust your boo, and trust your love. After all, it's better you allow your boo—who you've worked so hard to be with and waited so long and wished for so much—to get rid of a few unnecessary things than some other boo who comes after because you couldn't let go of a little porn. Besides, who has porn nowadays? Doesn't everyone just watch it online, on a private tab on an iPhone?
- No, no they don't. Pick your battles, gauge the importance of things and keep your eye on the bigger picture.

Chapter 74

Including, Introducing, and Proving Your Boo is Real

....

You've moved in, you're acquainted, you're comfortable on the home front, but now you're starting to feel another problem arising. It started fast and before you knew it, it became worse and worse.

Your friends text you for a night out like you're used to; your mom wants you to come over for dinner Sunday like you usually do; your boss wants you to stay extra hours like you usually do; your sister wants to go to dinner like you usually do; your nephew wants to go to the museum this weekend, or the water park or just do something fun like you usually do. But your boo wants to spend time with you. All the time.

Like. All. The. Freaking. Time.

Sure, you love it. It's like you've always wanted. Your boo can't get enough of you. He wakes you up at midnight for a little action, he wakes up in the morning and gives you a little surprise, too. And then you shower and he's right there, ready to go again.

It's a freaking dream you're living. He wants to spend every minute with you and you love it like you thought you would, but now you feel yourself being spread thin. You're pulled in all these different directions and you don't know what to do about it.

Going out with your girls is fun, but what about taking your boo to your favorite bar like you promised? Your mom wants Sunday dinner, but what about the last day off with your boo before the stressful work week starts? Your sister wants dinner, but what about that movie date you promised your boo? Your nephew wants to go out on Saturday, and no matter what he's getting it because he's the best, but what about your boo?

It's all about inclusion. Adding a new person into your life changes things. Like it or not, the status quo is changed and either you, your friends, your family or your boo has to put up with it. Like it or not, you have twenty-four hours in a day, and you have to sleep for at least ten of those, so you have to make some choices. And man, they're tough to make.

So your friends want to go on a crazy night out—no guys included—but your boo wants to go to that bar you've been talking about so much. You have to make a decision. Either drag your boo to that girls night (hey, he can be a cute wingman for your girls) or invite your girls to change plans and meet you at the bar. Either way, someone will be disappointed, but it's only the beginning.

This happens when you're used to having your relationship at the palm of your hand—your phone. But now that phone has turned into a person—a real, living and breathing person—who has needs and wants and he needs and wants you.

Whatever the case, if the people around you love you as much as they say they do, they'll want your happiness no matter what. So if that means that your boo stays at home, or goes to the bar with his new coworkers while you go out with your girls, then so be it. If that means you drag your boo along to your parent's house for Sunday dinner, then so be it. Your mom is crazy about meeting him anyway. Besides, she thought you made him up so it's the perfect time to prove her wrong, really. Your sister, too. Your cousins, too for that matter.

- *Hot Tip*: Including your boo into your life does not have to be stressful. At the very least, your friends and family most likely want to meet the man of your dreams, the man who's kept you crazy for the past year and a half. And your boo, well he probably wants to meet the people in your life too.
- So include, introduce, and prove everyone who thought he was fake wrong.

Chapter 75

The flip side: Getting Introduced, Getting Included, And Proving You're Real and Not Just A Booty Call

....

You're in a new town, your boo is loving and caring and everything you ever wanted. His mind is on the right things, he cares about the important things, he even brings you breakfast in bed. He's doing everything he can to make you feel loved and wanted, included and at home. He's even introduced you to his (cough) lovely friends. They thought you were fake or just a booty call that made the trip to another state to get some. You say, no. It's not like that. They can see that now.

He's including you in his life, he's introducing you to his friends, coworkers, neighbors. Luckily, his family lives in a different town miles and miles away so you don't have to go through that so soon, but you will—eventually.

Most likely your boo is trying his best to balance his love life (you) with his old life (his friends), and it'll be hard for him to make the switch from bachelor to having a live-in girlfriend. Making the time for you and his friends is where the art of life comes in, and he's trying. He really is. He's skipping the bar after work and coming straight home to give you a foot massage and feed you strawberries, he's taking you to dinner and showing you around town, he's taking you to the lake and showing you nature you've never seen. He's making time for his friends and work and you and mixing it all together.

He's making it all happen. He's introducing you, he's including you, and he's proving you're real.

- ◆ *Quick Tip*: It's okay to hate his friends. It's okay to just act nice, but really want to flip them off every time they come over with cheap beer wanting to play the stupid video games you've already gotten rid of. And when they realize what you've done to your boo, the change that has taken place, they will hate you too.

- ◆ *Reminder*: That is okay. Yoko Ono didn't take *no shit from no one*, and she got freaking John Lennon. And you aren't going to take shit either. Keep that in mind the next time they casually drop by for a round of poker with cigars and domestic beer. Because no one is smoking in your home, and yes, because you say so.
- ◆ That's your home now. Deal with it.

Chapter 76

Moving in Together
(Because at this Point, if You Don't You're Fucked)

....

If you read the Feeling At Home Away From Home and didn't feel like it applied, then this one is for you.

Let's get one thing straight. You've put in the time. You've put in the effort. Either your boo or you have moved states or cities or countries or continents. Whatever your situation, there's only one thing to worry about now.

Let's say you've been dating—long distance, of course—for a year, a year and a half, two years, *more*, and now he's moved or you've moved. That's an improvement. It shows commitment, it says you're serious about this shit. It says you're willing to let go of everything in your life and go for what you want. It says you're willing to let your boo into your life, that carefully guarded life. The life you've cleaned up and expelled all the snake friends, all the fake friends you made from your ride or die posse, all the nasty ex's, all the crap people that didn't cut it, and allowed your boo in. It takes guts, it takes courage. It takes commitment.

So now you find yourself including your boo into your life, or introduced into his life and town, yet you live in your own apartment, your own little bubble of life and space. Or you're afraid to let your boo move in because...what? Society? Or your friends? Or your mom who refuses to let you live in sin?

At this point you might as well live together and sleep in separate beds, because that's the message you're giving off.

You've done the hard work, you've done it. Living together is the ultimate goal here, because if you've been in a long distance relationship for a year or years or more, then you're pretty fucked if you're not ready to move in and make the commitment.

It's like being in a relationship (long distance or no) and not saying those three little words we all love to hear. It's wasting your time being unsure and cautious.

What's the end goal of dating, in general? Meeting your soulmate, sharing a life, a home, a world. And if you're not there by now, maybe you'll never be there and this has all been a waste of precious time. Life is too short to dwell in the what-ifs. Go for it, or not, but make your decision.

- *Hot Tip*: Think about The Wedding Planner. Drew Barrymore's character had been dating that rich douche for years before he popped the question, right? In the end, all she did was waste her time away with a man who cheated, dragged her along, and took so long to decide he really did want her (all for the wrong reasons, but still), and she ended up falling in love with Adam Sandler's character who was the complete opposite of her douchey boyfriend.
- Don't be Drew Barrymore on The Wedding Planner. If you feel like you're just

going along with the motions, maybe another more drastic change is warranted.

- *Quick Tip*: Like with anything, take the time to talk it out. If you're really feeling like you're being dragged and tossed around, talk it out. Chances are your boo is feeling the same. You never know if your boo is feeling just as apprehensive about bringing up the topic of moving in together. So take charge, go after what you want, and don't be afraid to talk it out!

Chapter 77

Getting Used to His Smell

....

You and your boo have been having a great time. You love the sweet things he does, you even love his cute snoring after he falls asleep. It's all fun and games until he comes home straight from the gym—without showering.

That's right, your boo has a nasty case of B.O. But what do you do? Do you run for the spray-on deodorant, or do you just sit there acting like you're not about to pass out?

Getting used to nasty smells can take time, and if you let it, those nasty smells can become so ingrained in your nose you eventually end up mistaking them for natural, every day odors until your mom comes over for a little unexpected chat and she pulls you to the side and tells you you've fucked up enormously because you've let your stinky boo go too long without proper hygiene education.

Wait, you didn't know you had to educate your perfect, strong, manly man about hygiene? Sister, you have another thing coming. It won't just be how to properly wash behind his crusty ears, it will also be the proper way to wipe his ass to prevent those skid marks because he's probably never heard of ass wipes.

Better yet, pretend he's a freaking baby and you have to teach him about the ways of life and flossing and where the dirty clothes go, and tongue brushing and clipping his freaking toenails more than once every six months, and even using q-tips the proper way.

You have to do the whole bit. All of it. Have a health class in your living room if you want to because you're probably going to need it.

- *Reminder*: Just because your boo doesn't know how to prevent skid marks on his boxers doesn't mean his dear mommy didn't teach him. It just means he's had plenty of years living the bachelor life that he got lazy and forgot how the world turns.
- So go ahead and teach him, and when you have a son, teach him too.
- Don't worry. His live-in girlfriend will teach him all over again when the time comes.

- *Quick Tip*: Unless you want to live a life of B.O. and bad breath, or crusty ears and claws on his feet, let him know that there are great things that wonderful people have invented to prevent smells and crust and skid marks. It will only offend for a little while, but in the end it'll help.
- You'll be endlessly happy and your nose will thank you, too.

Chapter 78

Making Him Pick up After Himself

································

You're not a mommy. Or maybe you are, but your little bundle of joy is not a six-foot man baby who doesn't know how to pick up after himself. You've told him where the socks go, his boxers, too. You've told him, a hundred times at least, where the dirty clothes go. Yet when you walk by the hallway, his clearly dirty, stinky black socks really do nothing to improve the look of the fresh new wooden floors.

In fact, blood rushes to your head and you contemplate rushing him with a fork to get him to understand where the dirty clothes go. But you don't because you value your freedom.

You're well aware that prison is no place you want to be because, let's face it, you're not tough enough and you're probably going to end up some butch lesbian's little bitch. So you skulk and try to come up with a plan that will make him once and for all clean up his freaking mess.

These thoughts of pure joy were much easier when he was miles away because it gave you time to chill, but nooooo, now you have to do it all yourself and quick.

Then your mind goes back to that psychology class you took in college, back to when that cute professor with the salt and pepper hair talked about cleaning up after his wife.

How did he do it, again? Oh, that's right. He didn't.

That's right. *He didn't*. He let her live in her own filth until it made her feel like the piece of shit she was and picked up after herself.

So you decide to try it out. I mean, telling him hundreds of times hasn't worked out in the past so something's gotta work, right? Lo and behold, when you walk down the hallway, they're gone, and when you open the hamper they're there. It's a hallelujah moment, a vision, an answered prayer.

He walks up behind you and puts his arms around you and he says sorry for leaving a mess, he's seen the error of his ways and vows to never do it again.

And you send a private little prayer to that psychology professor from years ago, because at least you learned something of value in his class.

♦ *Hot Tip*: Many of us will turn to different forms of punishment in desperation for a clean home or in an attempt to clean up only after oneself. Punishment, in any form (unless it's consensual and in the bedroom) is never okay, and never advised. So instead of using sex as leverage, or bodily harm as punishment, try making it fun. Run around the house naked until it's all cleaned up and shower to wash the grime from your bodies together, then have sex. Or wash the clothes together and have sex on the washer. Make it fun, make it like everything else in your lives: fun, sexy, and exciting.

- *Reminder*: Yes, we all don't have time to run around the house naked to make cleaning with our boo fun, but if you want a clean house and have set Sundays (or whatever day) as your clean day, you're going to clean anyway. So might as well get naked and enjoy it because you're going to clean one way or another. Might as well have fun doing it!

Chapter 79

The Truth About Making Love Every Night

....

When you're apart there's nothing you can think of for longer than twenty minutes besides having crazy sex with your boo. It's on your mind when you wake up, when you're in the bath, when you're at work, when you're at the bar, when you're hanging out with your besties—hell, even at church.

You swear up and down that as soon as you're together forreal you'll jump his bones every hour on the hour. And it comes to pass—at least the first few days. It's all sweaty sex and takeout, it's chocolate covered strawberries and the sixty-nine and body pretzel, it's about testing his stamina and breaking his record of ejaculations and the number of orgasms you have back to back, it's about eating in bed and not caring about anything else in the world. It's about everything you've ever imagined and more.

But whoever says it lasts longer than seventy-two hours is a lying sack of shit. I mean, the last twenty-four hours will most likely be nudging each other awake when the alarm you set on that very exciting first day goes off letting you know it's been four hours without sex—or cold pizza.

When you finally make it out of that filth-encrusted room you've been shacking up in, it'll be like An Interview With A Vampire the first time you see the sun, but you won't be cremated, you'll just want the sun to die. So reach for those extra dark sunglasses, because you'll need them.

- *Hot Tip*: There's no shame in slowing down on your sexy time. If anything, it only means you're human and need sleep. Like real sleep that isn't disrupted by an alarm that wakes you up every four hours for sex. So if you've slowed down a notch, don't fret! It will never be like it was before (dun dun dun), but it's okay.
- Soon you'll start having children and then your living hell will truly begin.
- Oh, and blanket hogging is totally normal. Deal with it.

- *Quick Tip*: If you're having sex twice a month, just please break up. You know when you're single you get laid more than that, and trust me, your mood swings need it. So do everyone around you a favor and break up, or get jiggy with it.
- It's either you have sex more—a lot more—or you call it quits. It's a charitable act, really, because trust me. No one wants to be near you when you haven't gotten any for two weeks.
- I mean, you think those mass shooters would be out there shooting innocent people if they could've been indoors getting freaky with a coed instead? I didn't think so. Don't be like those shooters. Get laid. You have a willing parter by your side.

Chapter 80

Planning the Future

....

If you're cheesy as hell, chances are you've already planned how many children you two will have and the names of your two boys and the lucky girl. You've even decided what they'll be wearing to the first day of Kindergarten and what college they'll be going to.

You're great planners when it's about the fun stuff. Your boo will be changing diapers and won't be waking you up during the night to feed your little bundle of joy. You even have a contract written up stating he will never, ever wake you up, signed and all. You need your beauty sleep, duh.

You'll obviously live in a small-but-not-so-small town and have the best looking kids your genes will allow, they'll have an unblemished GPA and great extracurricular activities from the time they turn five.

It's fun planning life when there are no obstacles in sight, but when it gets to the topic of marriage, both of you are silent. It's obvious you two want to be together, want to have a life together, you even want to make babies together.

Still, the topic of marriage gets you. It's just so, *committed*. Common law partner sounds sterile and fake, so no, not that either. So then what?

- *Hot Tip*: Marriage can be a scary thought, so planning for the future and talking about it can ease the fear you, your boo, or both may have. It's not the end of the world if you've both decided against it. Angelina Jolie and Brad Pitt were not married when they had their beautiful clan and not until years after did they tie the knot. (Author's note: They filed for divorce after I wrote this! Jeez, damn it.)
- So, if keeping it cool and casual is your thing, by all means. Just make sure your boo is on the same track.

- *Quick Tip*: So you want to get married, now what? The dream wedding on your mind is about to burst if your boo doesn't propose soon, and you don't know how to bring it up. You get to talking about children and your future but he's avoiding the marriage portion of life.
- Well, all you have to do is simply tell him you don't want children without a rock on that manicured finger. He'll be either relieved you won't be having children soon and neither will there be a wedding, or he'll be so excited to start a life with you he'll be planning and—more importantly—saving for that rock.
- And if you have children already, then—sorry, hunty. You're fucked.

Chapter 81

Enjoying Life

....

So you're not married, you don't have kids, and he's not showing signs of giving you either of those things either. You're bunched up and moody because all your friends are getting married and having babies, and here you are. Finally your boo has decided to move back after abandoning you, and now you're ready for the next step. But he seems happy right where he is. And it infuriates you.

How can he be happy when all your slutty friends are getting married before you? Remember Kimberly from fifth grade? Yep, married. Honeymooned in Hawaii just like you wanted to. Skank. Remember Destiny from middle school? That's right, married. Honeymooned in Chile. Bitch. Remember Hailey from high school? Yes! Even that super skank is now married and pregnant to top it off. She honeymooned in the Philippines with her banker husband because she's a slutty skank and always has been.

- *Hot Tip*: Pressure seems to be all around us at all moments. With the sometimes great—sometimes depressing—invention of social media, news about your friends, former friends, and school mates is readily available whether you want to see it or not. Chances are one of your friends is getting engaged or married or becoming a mom every day, and yet here you are.
- Don't fret! You're young, hot, and girl, you got you your man. Doesn't matter if you moved, if he's moved or if you have plans to moving closer, the point is you're on your way. Find happiness in your path, find the good in your life and focus on that.

- *Quick Tip*: Remember that kids are really the devil and the longer you can stall that whole mess the better. Think about all the sex you'll be having—disruption free—on the meantime.
- You're welcome.

Chapter 82

Living Proof Love Exists

....

You're a survivor. Just like your favorite Destiny's Child song. You've lived the bad, overcome the ugly, and stayed for the great ending. You made it. You're part of the lucky 30%. Your boo is lying next to you as you finish this chapter, and his calming breaths calm you too.

You are living proof love exists. You're living proof long distance relationships can overcome anything because they're strong, they're real, they're honest. It's the best love you've ever had and the most you've ever loved.

It wasn't easy, but it was worth it.

You did it.

Congratu-fucking-lations.

ISBN: 978-1-5390-6176-2

www.andiava.wixsite.com/loveanddistance.com

The material contained in this book is presented only for entertainment purposes. Although the author has made every effort to ensure that the information in this book was correct at press time, the author does not assume and hereby disclaim any liability to any party for any loss, damage, or disruption caused by errors or omissions, whether such errors or omissions result from negligence, accident, or any other cause.
(In other words, don't blame me for your break-up, damn.)

About the Author

Ava Rey is a long distance relationship expert, owner and blogger of <u>Love & Distance</u>, and all around lover. With personal long distance relationship experience that she has written about and others she has yet to write, she has advice, hope and love for us all. She currently lives in Las Vegas which is 989.1 miles, 13.41 hours by car, 2.40 hours by plane, and 1591.8022 km away from her boo. She lives with her three cats and pet armadillo.

You can follow her on Instagram, <u>@reyava</u>. (Please. Pretty please with sugar on top ;).

Find Ava on:

Blog: <u>Love & Distance</u>

Instagram: <u>@reyava</u>

Facebook: <u>facebook.com/reyavaa</u>

Email: <u>Reyava702406@gmail.com</u>

1. 1. Ferdman, Roberto A. "How the Chance of Breaking up Changes the Longer Your Relationship Lasts." Washington Post. The Washington Post, 18 Mar. 2016. Web. 03 June. 2016.
2. 2. Harden, Seth. "Long Distance Relationship Statistics." *Statistic Brain*. N.p., 2016. Web. 03 June. 2016
3. "CheapAir.com." CheapAir. N.p., 25 Feb. 2016. Web. 30 June. 2016.
4. "Migration/Geographic Mobility." - Calculating Migration Expectancy Using ACS Data. N.p., 29 Jan. 2015. Web. 15 June. 2016.

Made in the USA
Middletown, DE
28 March 2019